Middle Eastern and Mediterranean Food

TAL SMITH & NIRIT SABAN
Photography by Russell Smith

JACANA

DEDICATED TO OUR DARLING MOM, HAVA

CONTENTS

INTRODUCTION

Lunch at Sababa

Walk into Sababa and you step onto a blank canvas with a riot of colour at its centre. This is the buffet, bright with salads; some stained pink with roasted beetroot juice, others seasoned with freshly squeezed lemon juice or strewn with generous quantities of fresh herbs. Lunch here is not just a celebration of food, it's a celebration of life.

Sababa is a Cape Town kitchen and deli run by sisters Tal Smith and Nirit Saban. The Sea Point store is the original Sababa deli and catering HQ and in the City Bowl there is a deli with an eat-in option. The food has a distinctly Middle-Eastern slant, evidenced by the coconut-dusted date ball that comes with a latte, the sesame-flecked schnitzels and the smoothest, creamiest hummus (easily consumed by the tub) and by the bourekitas – dainty, domed pies containing cheese, spinach or silky, meltingly soft leeks.

Tal, the older sister, is the originator of the Sababa concept and it's a neat fit that her husband, Russell, is a highly regarded food photographer. Greater than the obvious culinary connection, is the value that husband and wife both place on quality and integrity; their marriage is a true meeting of minds. Together they have a son, Danyel, who at two is already showing his affinity for food; he is happiest with a wooden spoon in hand emulating the stirring that he sees in his mom's kitchens.

Tal opened her first outlet in St John's Piazza, Sea Point, in 2009 and is still based there. Join her for a coffee in the compact shopping centre and your conversation will be interrupted by passers-by, complimenting her catering at a recent Bar Mitzvah or asking whether there is any fried fish for Shabbat dinner. It is not unusual to see someone drop off a cherished Le Creuset casserole only to collect it later, magically filled with the chosen Sababa favourite for a dinner party.

And through it all, even on a Friday, when Sea Point is at its busiest, Tal is the island in the storm. Whether she's writing down an order for a regular client or arranging trays of hot paprika-grilled chicken or holding back on the black pepper in her chicken soup family recipe as a special request, she treats her customers as she

4

The way our grandmothers cooked – the way our paternal grandmother still cooks – means that there are no shortcuts. At Sababa we try to do the same. Obviously there are limitations – you can't be the best at everything – but we try to make everything as fresh as possible and fortunately, because we are busy, we cook fresh food every day. – Tal

would family. For Tal it's a simple fact of life; people have differing tastes.

On the other side of Signal Hill, younger sister Nirit manages Sababa's more recent addition. The City Bowl branch opened in 2011, catering for the busy lunchtime trade and a regular Thursday fan club who have turned 'falafel night' at Sababa into something of an institution. The shop is situated near the top of Bree Street and once Nirit has closed up for the day you might catch sight of her longboarding down this broad, historic road, recently regenerated by heart-led, owner-run businesses.

At the Bree Street Sababa, the daily lunch buffet entices a decidedly health-conscious crowd, comprising hipsters in skinny jeans or sometimes a local artist in an embroidered vintage Maxi dress or office workers in skyscraper heels taking their lunchboxes to go. The length of table out front is a welcoming feature and the communal dining it encourages mirrors the sense of family that is so important to both Tal and Nirit.

It's how the sisters would eat at home, helping themselves from a wide variety of different offerings served in generous quantities and sitting down to eat together with the people they love, sharing and enjoying what they have before them – and around them. This is the sense of togetherness that underscores everything about Sababa – and to understand it, you need to understand the Saban family.

Dinner with the Sabans

The front door to the Saban home opens right onto their kitchen. There's no hallway or reception room, just a straight line into the heart of the house. And on a Friday night, when the family gathers for Shabbat (the Jewish Sabbath dinner), their home may be filled with an ever-changing contingent of in-laws, friends or fellow Israelis but always present are Tal and her family, Nirit, brothers Ori and Ben and their parents, Hava and Herzl.

Hava's creamy complexion and ash blonde curls are in stark contrast to Herzl's deeply olive skin and well-defined brows. Both were born in Israel; she has Romanian ancestry, his heritage is Libyan. In 1948 Herzl's family moved from Libya's capital, Tripoli, to Israel where he spent his youth in tented transit camps before building the family house in which his mother, Toni Saban, still lives today.

The typical Saban Friday night menu is essentially a tribute to Toni, though it might be construed as a tribute to onions, garlic and tomatoes – key ingredients in Libyan cuisine. Italians settlers in Tripoli in the 17th century brought with them tomato-based sauces, simple methods and slow cooking. The courses – chraime, chicken soup, mafrum – are like stepping-stones through their family history, the meeting of two Jewish cultures: the Sephardim and the Ashkenazi.

The former are traditionally from North Africa and the Mediterranean and the latter from Eastern Europe. Nirit puts it another way, describing her father's people as 'fiery and spicy', both in their cooking and temperament – and her mother's as 'softer and more gentle'. In Judaism you follow your mother's religion, but if both parents are Jewish, you follow your father's traditions. So when Hava, who is Ashkanazi, married Herzl, a Sephardi, her mother-in-law taught her all she needed to know about Sephardi cooking.

Dishes like chraime, which is served as a starter: an elegant slice of salmon – a sign of more prosperous times – smothered in a vibrant paprika-garlic-lemon sauce. 'There are three heads of garlic in this,' she says, using her hands to indicate the size of the heads. Herzl shrugs, 'Then you don't need antibiotics!' Yet it's not sharp or overpowering, there is only the mellow depth of garlic cooked long and slow.

Chraime is followed by bowls of clear, golden broth, which represent Hava's mother, Golda Kahana. It is her homemade chicken soup recipe and the rising steam is perfumed with dill. Arranged in the centre of each serving are a single carrot, a pirogen (a half-moon of meat-stuffed puff pastry) and a cross-section of butternut – soft enough to yield to the slightest pressure from a spoon. Even while eating dinner the conversation turns to food. Nirit recalls with a dreamy expression how Golda would bake off swirly rolls of sweet kranz dough filled with spiced walnuts and jam, and make pasta parcels called varenikes stuffed with mashed potato and fried onions. She describes how Golda would patiently caramelise more onions in duck fat for spooning over and melting between the hot, cooked raviolis. 'It is such a lot of work,' says Hava, shaking her head. But never too much work for Golda to make them for her grandchildren.

The conversation and the soup are a momentary glimpse of the Ashakanazi repertoire, of the food Hava would have loved as a young girl, but in some ways cultural labels and recipes seem irrelevant to Hava. Family and feeding the people she adores are what give her life

Our paternal grandmother, Toni, is a phenomenal cook, as was our maternal grandmother, Golda. Toni only cooks Libyan food – she is very, very traditional, whereas Golda embraced an assortment of different cooking styles. I do remember Golda on the odd occasion, making things we weren't familiar with, like gefilte fish and pickled herring, so we were exposed to Ashkenazi cooking when we visited her but it was never part of our upbringing. We enjoyed North African, Mediterranean and Middle-Eastern cooking from an early age, but, aside from chicken soup, my mother never made an Ashkenazi dish in our home.

meaning – both of which transcend styles of cooking. And through her actions, she illustrates Herzl's words: 'Cooking is like anything, do it with your heart or don't touch it.'

For the main course Hava returns to an elaborate preparation learned from Toni: Mafrum. This is a time-consuming, multi-layered effort: first potatoes are fashioned into pockets and filled with fragrant, spiced mince, then they are dusted with flour and fried and, finally, there's the simmering in tomato sauce. Hava recounts how her mother-in-law would even make the accompanying couscous by hand, pressing it through a sieve. To this day, back home in Israel, Toni still dries her own chillies and garlic and makes her own pickles.

Ori describes his grandmother's hands – which have seen years of hard work raising six children – as 'bigger than mine and leathery!' When one of the children asks, 'Doesn't Gran buy couscous now, because she's too old to make it?' Herzl puts both his hands on the table and looks incredulous, 'My mother? Buy couscous in a box!' Laughter breaks out around the table; his family knows the answer.

Tal and Nirit may have tamed their use of garlic for Sababa but they remain true to their mother and grandmother in many other ways – sourcing the best raw ingredients possible and making whatever they can themselves. Sababa's hummus has never known a tinned chickpea, the chilli sauce is their own recipe – and their long-term goal is to bake their own pita pockets.

At Sababa their childhood is referenced by a few family classics on the chalkboard menu, but mostly through ethos and ingredients. The sisters seek out, and incorporate into their cooking, Israeli cucumbers, dates, fresh and dried figs, nuts and olives, wild herbs, spices like za'atar or pomegranates (from the tree growing in their parent's garden) – all little reminders of Israel.

In season, Herzl's homegrown pomegranates conclude the Friday meal together with trays of ice-cold grapes, cubed sweet melon and squidgy dates. As he peels back the reddish-brown skin of the pomegranate, painstakingly popping out the seeds so they are free of pith, he reminisces about his boyhood; gathering figs from trees growing wild on Herzliya Pituach. 'They were as sweet as honey,' he says, 'we lived such a simple, good life…'

The finale, accompanied by espresso and mint tea, is a slice of Nirit's home-baked babka – a puffy loaf of yeast dough rolled around oozy, dark chocolate. Ori, who has just picked up a bunch of grapes, holds them in mid-air and looks torn, 'Hmmm… suddenly I don't feel like fruit anymore.'

'When you go to my mother's house,' says Herzl, 'the first thing she says is, "What do you want to eat?" And the first thing she does is lay a table for you. For them [his parents] food is a big thing, because of the shortages experienced during the war.' And since food is seen as something so precious, when offered abundantly it's the greatest expression of love there is.

My maternal grandmother, Golda, passed away recently, but whenever the grand-children from South Africa visited her and my grandfather (at least once a year) there was always a feast. As soon as my grandparents knew we were coming, they would prepare for months on end, stocking up the freezer with all the things they knew we loved.

My gran would bake tiny, bite-sized cheese croissants for heating in their toaster oven to have with our morning coffee. They would do massive shopping sprees before we arrived, buying Medjool dates, all meaty and soft, and garinem (seeds in the shell), which they would toast and salt themselves. And every single day we were there they would cook. The food was unbelievable and even though you can make the same recipes here, the ingredients are never the same. Theirs taste different, it tastes better… it tastes like a holiday!

Obviously they don't eat that way every day, but it's very important to Israelis to entertain people with food and it's an insult if you don't eat. We used to have serious problems because we've got such a big family. Everybody wants to see you and we would try to fit in as many people as we could, but at every house you visit, you have to eat!

THE SABABA STORY

Tal's Story

I was born in Israel, the oldest of four siblings, and my parents moved to South Africa when I was three months old. Although I grew up in Cape Town, my immediate family maintained the same attitude towards food shared by my extended family in Israel – food has always been a big part of our lives, especially home cooking.

I can't remember us eating out much and when we did my father was inevitably disappointed – it was terrible taking him to restaurants because we knew he was going to tell us, '… your mother's [or grandmother's] food is so much better!'

The kitchen, from our first house to the house we live in now, has always been the heart of the home – if there were ever renovations, the kitchen would always be done first! For my parents it is the most important room because they see meal times as an opportunity to get together, to talk about the day and to spend time with each other.

Although Saturdays and Sundays were slightly more relaxed, there was never a chance of us not attending dinner – especially on Shabbat, the Jewish Sabbath which is celebrated every Friday night. I get excited about and really look forward to our Friday night get-togethers; it is the one day of the week that I know I will get to see my siblings, when we will all have a chance to catch up, and at the end of the evening we always go home full, tired and completely satisfied.

I found my way into the kitchen quite naturally and the way I learned to cook was by hovering around my mother, asking whether I could help, sometimes getting involved and other times just observing. Later, while completing my psychology honours degree I worked part-time as an au-pair for a caterer and it became very clear to me that my future lay in food.

My parents were very against the idea. Coming from a foodie home they understood that cooking is a demanding physical job with very long hours and a very hard choice. But I was adamant, and asked if they would loan me the money for a one-year chef's course to which they agreed.

I enrolled at The Culinary Academy and it was a 'helluva' year, very challenging at times, but I loved the course. I learned so much and it gave me a real understanding of basic cooking techniques. I had learned so much from my family, but it wasn't enough, and now in turn there is a lot that I was able to bring home to my family; things that they never knew how to make.

Next, I headed to London on a mission: To make money, pay my parents back and move on. I worked in a busy burger joint where I learned how to get food out fast, experiencing foodie highlights in between. One that really resonated with me was Yottam Ottolenghi's restaurant, Ottolenghi. As soon as I saw Ottolenghi's food I recognised it, it made sense to me. His approach is fresh and modern, but his heritage is similar to mine.

When I returned to South Africa, my parents wouldn't accept the money. They only wanted me to prove to them this really was what I wanted to do and that I was going to follow through. So I kept building my knowledge, first in Israel where I found a successful ex-New York City baker to teach me how to make pita – something I wanted to learn before leaving Israel – and back in Cape Town, where I worked for French *patisserie*, Bonapartes, baking choux puffs, macarons and quiche Lorraine.

Then The Neighbour Goods Market at the Biscuit Mill started – it was booming – and I thought I could do something there that was more my style. The falafels,

sababa
Middle Eastern & Mediterranean
food prepared fresh daily
in our Kitchen!!

a family recipe handed down from my dad's side of the family, were an obvious choice. It was something I felt very confident about and I knew how to make everything involved. My sister Nirit was in Cape Town at the time and she was keen to help.

But someone else had already cornered the pita market, so we decided to do a spread of the slow-cooked Mediterranean-Middle-Eastern foods with which we were so familiar – stuffed peppers, stuffed cabbage rolls, mafrum, hummus, which we were selling tub after tub! It was basically a mini Sababa. When Nirit returned to Israel, I needed to find a more practical solution. Fortunately the market had grown and I finally got the go-ahead to set up a falafel stand.

The longer I was at the market, the more people asked me to supply them with what I was selling there. I set up falafel and shwarma stands for parties and as a result of those jobs I began offering all the other things I knew how to make but wasn't selling at the market. Catering was where I was headed and it remains a big part of our business today.

It was also through the market that I met Pete Goffe-Wood whom I worked with for about a year, while maintaining my Saturday falafel stand. It was an incredible experience. I think he's one of the best chefs ever; he's down-to-earth but so knowledgeable and super-confident in the kitchen. With him I learned that you don't have to be an arrogant chef for people to work well for you; that you can make a kitchen a fun environment in which to work.

One Saturday I was approached about selling my falafels in a shop that had come up for rental in St John's Piazza. There was no harm in having a look. When I saw the space I could immediately picture what I was going to do with it – and it wasn't going to be a falafel shop! It would be something small where I could offer all those things we sold at the Biscuit Mill in the very beginning, but done in a clever way. And that is how Sababa Sea Point began.

'Sababa' is slang in Hebrew. It doesn't have a specific translation but if somebody says something positive, you respond with 'Sababa!' – meaning 'awesome', 'cool', 'terrific', 'great', 'sure'. Most people use it and I don't think you'll have a single conversation in Israel, without hearing 'Sababa'. My maiden name is Saban, so I liked the Saban-Sababa connection.

I always knew I wanted to do something on my own and something with an Israeli flavour. And Sababa is very much how we eat at home, congregating around a feast at one big table, helping ourselves to good-quality, fresh, healthy food that's uncomplicated. At Sababa we serve the wholesome food people want to eat but don't necessarily have the time to make themselves.

My father shopped around with me to find the equipment we needed and a very good friend, Jaco van Rensburg, helped me define Sababa's entire look and feel – from branding down to details like song playlists. Jaco knows how to make everything look good. I wanted the food to be the focus so we chose a clean, neutral background, which would make all the colours on the buffet stand out, bringing in elements symbolic of the Middle East – like the marble, which is used in Middle-Eastern countries to keep rooms cool.

Jaco and I planned where every single bowl and platter was going to be placed for the opening week and what was going to go on them, visualising how everything would fit on the table by arranging cut outs of the dishes on the floor. I had pages and pages of salad ideas and ingredient combinations but knew that the initial array needed to be very visual, with varying colours and textures – it needed to draw people in – criteria we still use when making our selections.

When I look at my menu notes from when we opened, the salads we served are still very much a part of Sababa, like the marinated beetroot with carrots, green beans, toasted sunflower seeds and wild rocket, the shredded cabbage with sesame and balsamic dressing, the aubergine with green beans, mangetout and asparagus with origanum dressing. (All of these recipes are in this book.)

Then I had two months and found two women who would work with me, Florence Anta and Vuyiseka Nolenze. I trained them every day in the flat that Russell and I were living in at the time, so Russell tasted most of the testing! When we were ready Florence and Vuyi only knew a quarter of what they know today, but it was enough for us to start. I opened the shop, with just the two of them and me, and… it was busy!

Suddenly I had to be the front of house person and the chef in the kitchen. For the opening day we prepared as much as we could the night before, but then we sold out and had to start all over again! So I called on family; my mom worked in the shop, my brother Ben worked in the shop. It was Ben who came up with the idea of offering a lunch box (one main and three salads) at a set price, when he saw that customers wanted to create a meal for themselves.

The amazing thing about Sababa is that, except for one person, all the people who work with me at Sababa have worked with me since day one. They're a brilliant team and their work is better than a lot of professionals that I've worked with in the past. They're a huge part of the business and the truth is I wouldn't be able to do it without them.

I'll never forget our first falafel night. We advertised and told all our friends but we didn't think everyone was going to come. It was mayhem! About 300 people arrived and people were queuing around the block to buy the falafels. – Tal

I purposefully kept the kitchens open plan in both shops so that our staff would get the recognition they so much deserved. Now customers just walk straight into the kitchen and ask, 'Oooh what's cooking in this pot?' and I always see how the kitchen staff enjoy the compliments they receive, just as I had enjoyed that instant feedback while selling falafals at the market.

When Nirit came back from Israel we decided to do something together. Initially it wasn't at all Sababa, it was something totally different, but at the Sea Point shop people kept saying, 'I wish you had a little table where I could sit and eat my lunch, somewhere that's more of a restaurant.' So one day I said, 'Why don't we do Sababa again?'

It made sense to open another Sababa with someone I trusted and with whom I had worked well in the past. We found a space in town and shortly afterwards signed the lease. Bree Street hadn't really been 'discovered' yet but I've always believed, as long as your food is good, people will find out about you and come, so it doesn't really matter where you are.

Nirit's Story

I have always been a cook, and I have always known I was going to cook. Food is a basic human need and people have to eat – it is a necessary physical process – and the simple act of eating brings people together and is unifying. That is why I believe in what I do.

I worked with Tal when we did the market, back in the day, when the Biscuit Mill had just started. We did it together but Tal had very clear ideas in mind and she was the one leading us. Then we went on holiday to Israel and I remained there, working for two-and-a-half years accumulating experience, while Tal carried on without me in Cape Town.

At that point I'd lost all faith in restaurants but when I started working at Segev in Herzliya, it opened my eyes and put me right back on the train. The work environment was highly professional and each person there was in their mind and soul a chef. The quality of the ingredients, because it is a fine-dining restaurant, were always of the highest standard and each dish looked like a picture – it was beautiful.

There were natural liquorice-scented sticks to skewer lamb with before roasting it in the taboun (similar to a pizza oven), and a winner of a salad, all spiky and coral-pink. There were radishes – the radishes in Israel are like apples – and kohlrabi, julienned to the size of the big braai matchsticks, mixed with home-made sweet-chilli mayonnaise, black sesame seeds, fresh ginger, a whole bunch of fresh coriander, and smashed wasabi peas and toasted cashews.

Everything was made to order. When I worked in the dessert section we had our own little oven, so everyone received the most crisp, freshest possible tuille on their plate. I felt this was the way things should be in a restaurant and it was like school all over again. My intention was to learn everything I could and, even though I was getting paid for it, this was my real education.

Next, I had my heart set on working for the Dallal Bakery in Neve Tsedek. I waited for four months to get a job there because nothing spoke to me like Dallal did and if I have something in my mind I just cannot accept anything else. I was up at 4.00 am every morning because work started at 6.00 am. I'm not a morning person so it really proved how much I wanted to be there.

Dallal taught me about precision and discipline – it's a bakery so you have to be precise about what you do. Even though I've always been very careful about taste, the way I get there is quite fluid and free. Dallal gave me a reason to be meticulous in my process – because then things generally turn out as they should. And that's where I learned how to make traditional rugelach and babkas.

Although I went to the same chef school as Tal, a much greater influence was definitely my home – just being in the kitchen with my mom and my dad – because that's where all the love is. After adding professional experience everything started to feel right but I still believed in what they showed me, that it was a good base, and that I needed to stay true to what they had shared with me.

When I came back to Cape Town, Tal had launched Sababa Sea Point and it made sense to expand on that. Ever since Tal and I worked at the market, I was sure we would do something else together. We are all about home, family, cooking – there was always going to be us as a unit.

We had something good to share and basically I wanted to share the love! We happened to be walking along Bree Street one day and saw the space where we are now situated. I was so confident this area was going to accept Sababa. I saw all the buildings filled with people working in the area and thought: 'Ah! They need food – good food!' It's primal.

The Bree Street team is phenomenal; we've created a family there as well – a family within a family. We get to know our customers on a personal level and their appreciation for what we do validates us. For me, Sababa is about creating our own legacy with what we've already been given.

SEASONING & STOCK

Seasoning

Seasoning correctly is a key factor in producing delicious food and although we've given measurements for salt, pepper and other spices, they are only a guide. At Sababa the ingredients we use are never the same. The tomatoes will differ from day to day even though we use them all year round but the way we season when we cook them, adjusting salt or sugar accordingly, keeps a dish consistent.

If ten people follow a standard recipe, it's likely not one dish will taste the same. There is a sense of touch or feel that a good cook has, which makes each person's food unique to them. And you can develop a feel for seasoning. We tell our staff all the time to taste the food as they cook to achieve that perfect balance. You don't want to under-season because then you're not maximising your ingredients or to over-season because then you're killing flavour.

While we're on the subject, people also seem worried about having too much salt in their diet – we hear it all the time at Sababa. We add salt to pretty much everything but we strongly believe if you're cooking from scratch, adding a bit of salt and pepper here and there, it can't be bad for you. It's the processed foods, the food you're not actually making yourself that you need to be worried about.

Salting meat

We marinate a lot of our meat overnight but we only add salt just before we're about to cook it. Adding salt the day before will draw out the all the meat's juices, leaving it dry.

Seasoning beans and pulses

When boiling beans and pulses avoid adding salt to the cooking water as it toughens the skins – rather season once they are cooked.

Spices

We know it's not always practical or available in South Africa but if you can buy freshly ground spices or grind your spices just before using them, you will get a cleaner, more potent flavour.

Stock

When using chicken or vegetable stock, we prefer the Telma brand from Israel, which is available locally.

MEZZE & DIPS

PUTTING TOGETHER A MEZZE PLATTER

A good platter will have six or more different mezzes served with pita bread or laffa (an Iraqi flatbread). Here are some of the things we would put together:

- *Hummus* is always top of our list, either as it is or with tahina. The way I like to present it is with tahina in the centre of the plate and the hummus surrounding it. That way, when you dip your bread, you get both the hummus and tahina along with the paprika, za'atar, pine nuts or whatever else you've used as a garnish.
- *Olives and pickles* – always olives and pickled vegetables like carrot, beetroot, cauliflower and turnips. (Obviously the best you can get.)
- Then definitely an *aubergine* dish of some sort – either pickled or fried, or with tomato, tahina or mayonnaise.
- A *fresh salad*, typically an Israeli chopped salad.
- Marinated or pickled *peppers*.
- Moroccan *carrot salad*.
- Some kind of *tomato salad*, like letcho or matboucha.
- And always *chilli sauce* of some kind.

We often suggest adding dolmades but it's not something you're likely to find on a mezze platter in Israel. You'll definitely want to add them – or even some falafel balls or shredded lamb or haloumi cheese – if you're having the mezze platter as a main meal.

Falafels and dolmades are not practical to make at home and we have not included recipes for them. Dolmades are time consuming to make. Falafels involve a complicated process using machinery most people would not have at home.

A note on olives
With almost every Israeli meal you'll get a small ramekin of olives, and olives together with hummus is particularly good. We struggle to find good olives, so last year an Israeli friend taught me how to make my own. The juicy texture and good flavour is definitely worth the trouble and I would recommend that anyone who loves olives as much as we do, make their own.

HUMMUS

The best hummus we ever tasted was at a traditional Libyan restaurant called Rachmo but there are hummus shops and cafés all over Israel, especially in the Arab villages. They're called hummusias and the hummus is served steaming hot, topped with slow-cooked chickpeas or broad beans, or faul (also a kind of broad bean), or even with some shredded lamb. There is pita on the side but that is lunch or dinner, not just a dip.

Hummus must be one of the healthiest things a person can eat. It's full of protein from the chickpeas and good oils from the tahina and Sababa's hummus was one of the first things I fed Danyel when he went onto solids! There are many variations on hummus made in many different places and where it's made generally determines how much tahina is added. Israeli hummus is more tahina based and at Sababa we like to use a lot of tahina too.

At Sababa we also cook our chickpeas from scratch. Tinned chickpeas not only taste acidic, they give the hummus a grainy texture because the chickpea skins are still intact. So we soak fresh, dried chickpeas overnight and then cook them very slowly for a very long time. We add bicarb to the water, which helps to release the skins from the chickpeas which then rise to the surface so you can just skim them off the top.

By the end of cooking you should be left with very, very soft chickpeas that are almost falling apart. The trick is not to cook them until they break down completely, otherwise you'll have chickpea soup, but you do want a very soft centre. Then you drain the chickpeas in a colander and blend them up with tahina, lemon juice, garlic and salt – no olive oil.

Tahina is basically pure sesame oil so there's no need to mix oil into the hummus. Instead, by drizzling a special extra-virgin olive oil over the top you will actually be able to taste it, and appreciate its green, peppery flavours against the hummus. We top our hummus with fresh extra-virgin olive oil and za'atar, which also gives it a citrusy bite. Some people add paprika for decoration and pine nuts are also a delicious addition.

- 500 g dried chickpeas
- 2 tsp bicarbonate of soda
- 6 cloves garlic, crushed
- 1 cup fresh lemon juice
- 3 cups tahina paste
- 1 tsp salt
- 200 ml hot water
- 1 tsp cumin (optional)

Soak the chickpeas overnight using 3 times the amount of water with 1 tsp of bicarbonate of soda. Strain the chickpeas through a colander and rinse them under cold water. Boil the chickpeas in a pot with double the amount of water and 1 tsp of bicarbonate of soda and cook until the chickpeas are soft and almost falling apart.

Strain the chickpeas and allow them to cool slightly. Then blend the chickpeas with the rest of the ingredients until smooth.

TAHINA

Tahina is one of those ingredients that are always in our cupboard as a pantry staple and usually also on our dinner table. In Israel it's found everywhere from take-away falafel shops to fine-dining restaurants and it can be used in all kinds of ways. It's made of sesame seeds ground to a smooth paste and there are different varieties. Some of the darker varieties, for instance, are made with sesame seeds that have been toasted before they are crushed. Israelis argue about which is the best quality but we think it is simply a matter of personal taste.

Tahina in its pure form is a paste but it can be thinned out slightly with water or lemon juice to become a thickish sauce (which is the way we use it as a condiment) or it can be thinned out until very runny and used as a dressing. It's even used in desserts and sweet baking recipes, like our sesame biscuits – very yummy!

At Sababa we sell tahina as a dip, we spoon it over falafels, schnitzels and shwarmas and use it to dress vegetables. We also sell jars of tahina paste, which we import by the container load. We source an organic tahina from Israel because the tahina available here is not as good – it seems to be diluted.

It is quite funny watching our customer's tahina consumption. The average South African will buy a jar from us and it will take them a good four to five months to use it up. Then we've got the Israelis, who are like us in that they use it as part of every meal and a small jar would probably only last two days – they buy it by the drum!

We bring tahina in from Israel in bulk and sell it in one-litre jars and 18 kg drums. To purchase, please contact us on +27 (0) 21 433 0570 or +27 (0) 21 424 7480.

Tahina Sauce

- 250 ml tahina paste
- 125 ml water
- 2 lemons, juiced
- 3 cloves garlic, crushed
- 2 ml salt

Combine all the ingredients together in a bowl and mix well until smooth. We like our tahina to be quite thick but if you prefer it more runny or want to use it as a dressing then add a little more water and mix through.

Makes about 300 ml

Cook's Note
The ingredients are best combined using a hand whisk or small hand blender.

AUBERGINES

The aubergine is our favourite vegetable – it is so versatile. In Israel they use aubergines to bind meatballs for a light, moussy texture and we even make aubergine schnitzels. I also find it's one of those vegetables that are actually filling and satisfying. So we're always trying out new ways to cook with aubergine, to introduce it to our customers.

A lot of people say they don't like aubergines or that they get an unpleasant sensation on their tongue after eating them – some even say they're allergic but we know that's not true. It might have been bitter or acidic because the aubergine wasn't salted properly or maybe it wasn't ripe enough or was still raw – there's nothing worse than half-cooked aubergine, it's like eating a hard sponge!

When customers do taste one of our aubergine dishes, they often say, 'This is the best aubergine I've ever had!' Usually, it's because most people don't know how to prepare it. Yet it's not a complicated vegetable to cook. Mostly we bake it (although it is very nice fried as well) and we find the best technique is to brush the aubergine with a little oil so it gets just the right amount for the perfect texture without soaking up so much that it becomes slimy.

Selecting the best aubergine

The skin must be smooth and they must feel firm. The aubergine mustn't be too heavy because if it's heavy it means it has a lot of seeds. And medium-sized are best – for some reason the larger ones seem to be more bitter.

Salting aubergines

This has become a habit in our cooking; we were taught from an early age that this is a necessary step to draw out any bitterness. But on the odd occasion when we've been working with vast quantities of aubergines – too many to salt – or simply haven't had the time, they've turned out fine. I've heard people say it's because aubergines today have been modified to eliminate bitterness but we've noticed that salting still makes some difference even though modern varieties of aubergine may not be as bitter as the ones our grandmothers used to buy.

To salt aubergines, slice, arrange in a colander and sprinkle with salt. The salting period can range from 10 or 15 minutes to an hour, to a full day, depending on how much time you have. Overnight is best – if you can afford it – but even after five minutes you will see small droplets of moisture collecting on the flesh. Before using the aubergines simply wipe off all the moisture using a clean tea towel or rinse under cold water.

Roasting aubergines

Cut the aubergines into wedges, salt them as described above and then wipe clean. Arrange on a baking sheet with about 2 cm between them and brush both fleshy sides of each wedge – I brush one side, turn that side flat onto the baking sheet and then brush the other side. Season with salt and pepper and roast the aubergines at 180°C for about 30 minutes or until soft on the inside and nicely browned on the outside.

Charring aubergines

Charring aubergines over hot coals is the best way to get a smoky flavour. You want to char them well – until blackened all over – which is why we refer to it as burning the aubergines. After you've removed all the burnt, crispy skin, place them on a strainer while they cool. That way any liquid will drain out and all you're left with is the smoky aubergine flesh.

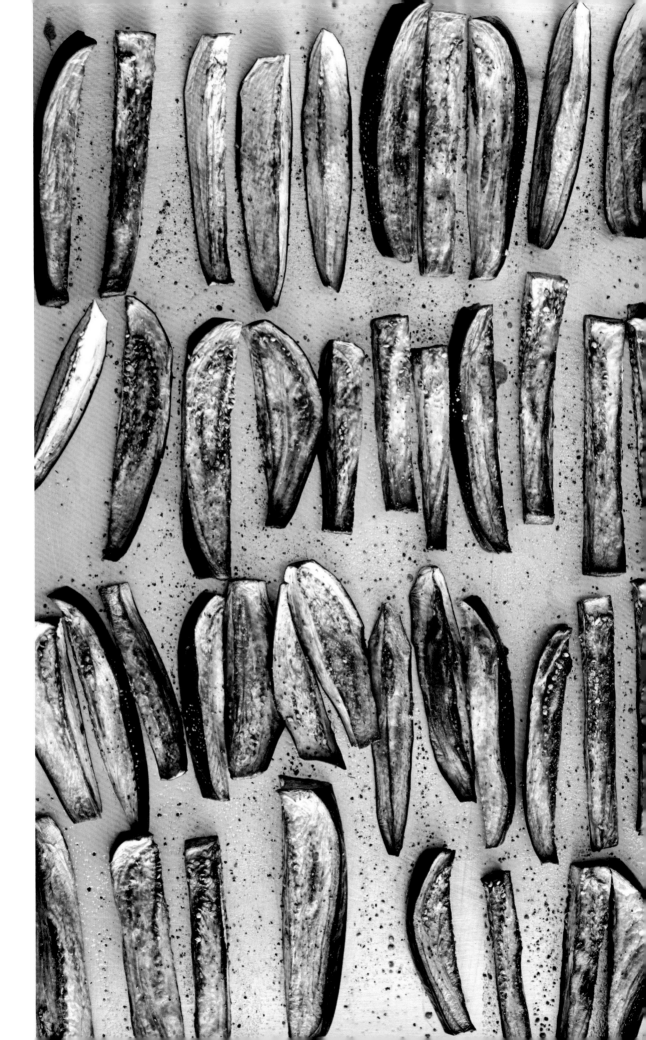

Baba Ganoush

A classic combination of aubergine and tahina, two ingredients which always work so well together.

- 2 medium aubergines
- 1 lemon, juiced
- 2 cloves garlic, crushed
- 4 tbsp tahina
- salt to taste

Cook's Note
If you are pressed for time, simply roast the aubergines as explained in the section Roasting Aubergines and blend with the remaining ingredients until smooth.

The best way to prepare the aubergines for this dip is to cook the aubergines on an open flame until charred. Remember to keep turning the aubergines on the grill so that they cook evenly. Once black all over, remove them from the heat and allow them to cool for a while. Remove the charred skin and leave to drain on a colander.

Cut the aubergines into chunks and then blend together with the tahina, lemon juice, crushed garlic and a pinch of salt. You can add some water at this stage if you prefer a thinner consistency.

Makes about 250 ml

Aubergine Schnitzels

This is a great option for vegetarians.

- 3 medium aubergines
- 250 ml breadcrumbs
- 125 ml sesame seeds
- pinch salt and freshly ground black pepper
- 3 eggs
- oil for frying

Cut the aubergines into approximately 1 cm thick slices. Salt the aubergines and leave them for about 20 minutes so that any bitterness will be released. Rinse the aubergines under cold water and then dry them with a clean cloth.

Prepare the breadcrumb mixture by mixing together the breadcrumbs with the sesame seeds and a pinch of salt and pepper.

Heat the oil in a frying pan. Once the oil is hot, take the aubergine slices and dip them first into the egg and then into the breadcrumbs. Then fry the aubergines in the oil for about 2 minutes on each side, until the slices are soft on the inside and the outside is crisp and golden brown.

Serves 6 - 8

MEZZE-STYLE SALADS

Whenever we have these mezze salads over big festivals, my dad char-grills boxes full of peppers – really, he goes through boxes and boxes of vegetables! We used to wonder, how much can six people actually eat? But his thinking is, it takes time so if you're going to do it, do it in bulk. He's right, and as these salads are either pickled or marinated, they will last for quite a while once they're made. Marinate the peppers and aubergines to taste – the way we like them is with loads of garlic and a lot of vinegar.

Aubergines in Vinegar

- 2 large aubergines
- 5 cloves garlic, thinly sliced
- 1 cup spirit vinegar
- 1 cup warm water
- 1 tsp salt
- oil for frying

Cut the aubergines into slices about 1 cm thick. Sprinkle them with salt and leave them to rest for an hour. Then using some paper towels wipe each slice dry. Heat some oil in a frying pan and fry the aubergine slices until golden brown. Leave them to cool on paper towel so that any excess oil can be absorbed.

In the meantime combine the vinegar with warm water and salt. Layer the aubergines in a dish with a slice of garlic on each slice of aubergine. Cover the aubergines with the pickling liquid and leave them in the fridge to marinade overnight before serving.

This dish will last 2 – 3 weeks in the fridge.

Serves 10 – 12

Marinated Peppers in Vinegar

- 6 red peppers
- 6 yellow peppers
- 375 ml warm water
- 375 ml spirit vinegar
- 125 ml vegetable oil
- 10 cloves garlic, halved

Char the peppers on an open flame or on the braai until the skins are blackened.
When cooked, place them in a closed plastic bag to steam for about 20 minutes.
Peel the skin off, remove the seeds and wash under cold running water. Cut the peppers into quarters or strips.

Combine the warm water with the vinegar and salt.

Place the peppers in a dish with the garlic between each layer. Pour the liquid over the peppers and then cover the top with vegetable oil. Once the dish has cooled down completely, leave it in the fridge overnight before serving.

This dish will last 3 – 4 weeks in the fridge.

Serves 10 – 12

Marinated Peppers with Lemon

- 5 red peppers
- 5 yellow peppers
- 3 cloves garlic, crushed
- 4 lemons, juiced
- 1 cup extra virgin olive oil
- salt to taste

Char the peppers on an open flame or on the braai until blackened. Once they are ready, place them in a plastic bag to steam for about 20 minutes. Remove the skin and seeds and wash the peppers under cold running water. Cut the peppers into quarters or strips.

Combine the garlic with the lemon juice, olive oil and salt. Place the peppers in a dish, pour the liquid over and mix everything together.

Leave to cool and then keep the dish in the fridge overnight before serving.

This dish will last a month in the fridge.

Serves 10 – 12

Moroccan Carrot Salad

Typically made with caraway seeds, this version learned from our mom is slightly different. It has all the cumin-garlic-paprika flavours so much loved by my dad's side of the family and over festivals we eat it with pickled aubergines, marinated peppers, tahina, hummus and pita.

- 7 - 8 cloves garlic, crushed
- 80 ml spirit vinegar
- 1 tsp salt
- 2 ml sweet paprika
- 2 ml cayenne pepper
- 1 tsp cumin
- 60 ml vegetable oil
- 500 g carrots, peeled and cut into rounds
- handful Italian flat-leaf parsley, chopped
- handful coriander, chopped

Mix together the garlic, vinegar, salt, paprika, cayenne pepper, cumin and oil.

Bring a pot of water to the boil and cook the carrots until they just begin to soften.

Strain the carrots through a colander and then put them back in the pot with the spice mixture.

Mix everything together on a low heat for about a minute and then turn the heat off.

Add the chopped herbs and mix through.

Once this salad has cooled down it is ready to serve.

Serves 4 - 6

Letcho

This Eastern-European salad recipe from our maternal grandmother contains peppers, onions, tomato and paprika, cooked slowly in a pan until beautifully sweet. It balances the stronger dips and sauces usually found on a mezze platter.

- 2 tbsp sunflower oil
- 2 onions, sliced
- 3 yellow peppers, sliced
- 3 red peppers, sliced
- 3 cloves garlic, sliced
- 1 tbsp tomato paste
- 1 tbsp sugar
- pinch salt and freshly ground black pepper
- 150 ml water

Fry the onions until soft and translucent. Add the peppers and cook for about 3 minutes until they soften. Add the garlic, tomato paste, sugar, salt, pepper and water.

Cook for a further 15 - 20 minutes on a low heat. Adjust the seasoning if necessary.

Serves 4 - 6

Cook's Note
For a bit of a kick, add one sliced red chilli.

DIPS

Matbucha

A cooked tomato dip, which comes from our dad and is best served as a mezze and eaten with bread.

- 2 tbsp sunflower oil
- 1 onion, finely diced
- 4 large ripe tomatoes, chopped
- 1 green pepper, diced
- 1 red chilli, sliced
- 3 cloves garlic, sliced
- 250 ml water
- 2 tbsp sugar
- 2 ml salt and a pinch of freshly ground black pepper

Fry the onions in oil until soft and translucent. Add the rest of the ingredients and cook on a low heat for 20 – 30 minutes until reduced to a third of what you started with and have a thick consistency.

Serves 4 – 6

Cook's Note
Be sure to use ripe or, better still, over-ripe tomatoes.

Tzatziki

This is more of a Greek-style dip and although it's not traditionally eaten with falafels in Israel we offer it with our falafels because we enjoy the freshness it provides.

- 1 large English cucumber
- 500 ml Greek yoghurt
- 2.5 ml salt
- 3 cloves garlic, crushed

Deseed the cucumber and grate it finely. Mix the cucumber and the yoghurt, salt and garlic. Leave in the fridge for an hour before serving.

Makes about 500 ml

Smoked Salmon Dip

- 500 g smoked Norwegian salmon
- half a red onion, chopped
- 100 g gherkins, chopped
- 200 g full fat cream cheese
- 2 lemons, zest and juice
- 40 g dill, chopped
- 160 ml cream
- salt and freshly ground black pepper to taste
- 1 ml extra virgin olive oil for serving
- za'atar for serving

Break the salmon into pieces and place in a food processor. Add the rest of the ingredients and blend everything together until just combined. To serve, drizzle olive oil, sprinkle over some za'atar and serve with bread or crackers.

Makes 1 litre

Smoked Snoek Dip

- 200 g smoked snoek
- half a red onion, diced
- handful Italian flat-leaf parsley, chopped
- 2 spring onions, chopped
- 100 ml cream
- 3 tbsp mayonnaise
- salt and freshly ground black pepper to taste
- 1 lemon, zest and juice
- extra virgin olive oil for serving
- extra fresh chopped Italian flat-leaf parsley for serving

Shred the snoek making sure you get rid of all the bones. Using a hand blender, blend the rest of the ingredients together. Mix the snoek in by hand and then leave the mixture in the fridge for an hour before serving. To serve, drizzle with some olive oil and sprinkle with some extra freshly chopped parsley.

Makes about 600 ml

Tuna, Chilli and Lemon Dip

- 150 ml cream
- 480 g tinned tuna
- 2 ml smoked paprika
- pinch of chilli powder
- 2 green chillies, deseeded and chopped
- 200 g full fat cream cheese
- 2 lemons, zest and juice
- 2 spring onions, chopped
- half a red onion, diced
- 20 g dill, chopped
- 20 g Italian flat-leaf parsley, chopped
- 2 tsp olive oil
- salt and freshly ground black pepper to taste
- extra virgin olive oil for serving
- extra finely chopped Italian flat-leaf parsley for serving

Mix all the ingredients together in a bowl. Leave the mixture in the fridge for an hour to set slightly. When serving, add some extra finely chopped Italian parsley and a drizzle of extra virgin olive oil.

Makes 1 litre

SOUPS

In winter we have soup every night. It has always been our first course, to warm us up. Today our mother still serves soup as part of the evening meal even though many of her soups, like the minestrone, have everything in them – veggies, beans, pulses – so you don't actually need much more to eat!

Most of these recipes came from our mom, who taught us to start a soup by sweating off onions and celery (there must always be celery!) before adding the rest of the ingredients. At chef's school we learned the base should also include onion, celery and carrot but my mother's method is so ingrained in me, so sometimes we add carrot but not always.

Lentil and Sweet Potato Soup

This is one of our mom's hearty and healthy soups, thickened with split lentils.

- 2 tbsp vegetable oil
- 2 onions, roughly chopped
- 1 bunch celery, chopped
- 250 g split lentils
- 800 g sweet potato, cubed
- 3 tbsp vegetable stock powder
- 1 tsp salt
- 2 ml freshly ground black pepper

Sweat the onions and celery with the oil in a soup pot until soft and translucent.

Add the rest of the ingredients, mix through and then fill the pot with 3 litres of water.

Bring to the boil and then simmer for about an hour, stirring every so often so that the split lentils don't stick to the bottom of the pot. If the soup thickens too much, add a little water.

Serves 8 – 10

Chicken Soup

Chicken soup is very much a part of Jewish Ashkenazi culture. It's eaten on Friday nights (Jewish Sabbath) and on festivals, and during Passover we add little Matzo dumplings called kneidlach. The way we were taught by my mom, who was taught by her mom, is to use the chicken wings (and neck if you can find it) because they are the most flavoursome parts and my gran's special touch is to add dill.

- 6 chicken wings
- 2 potatoes, peeled and halved
- 1 onion, peeled and quartered
- 2 baby cabbages, halved
- half bunch table celery, cut into 5 cm long pieces
- 1 medium sweet potato, peeled and cut into large chunks
- 2 carrots, peeled and cut into large chunks
- 300 g baby marrow, peeled and cut into large chunks
- 250 g butternut, peeled and cut into large chunks
- 4 tbsp chicken stock
- salt and freshly ground black pepper to taste
- handful chopped dill

Fill a pot with 7 litres of water. Add the chicken wings and bring the water to the boil.

While the pot is heating up, all the fat from the chicken will rise to the surface and this can be easily removed with a large spoon. Allow the water to boil for 10 – 15 minutes and then add the rest of the ingredients. Fill the pot with water and boil on a medium heat for about an hour. Test the seasoning and add more salt and pepper if necessary.

Serves 10 – 12

Cook's Note
Be sure to skim off all the fat and foam that rises up to the surface before the broth comes to the boil.

Pea and Barley Soup

A thick, wintery soup with the nuttiness of barley, learned from my mom.

- 125 ml vegetable oil
- 2 onions, diced
- 1 bunch table celery, sliced
- salt and freshly ground black pepper to taste
- 3 tbsp vegetable stock powder
- 350 g split peas
- 250 ml barley
- 3 – 4 litres water

Sweat the onions in the oil until they soften. Add the celery and continue cooking till soft. Add salt, pepper, stock, split peas, barley and 3 litres of water. Bring the soup to the boil and then cook on a low heat for about 40 – 60 minutes. Stir occasionally so that the peas don't stick to the bottom of the pot. The soup is ready once all the peas have dissolved. You might need to add more water if the soup thickens too much.

Serves 8 – 10

Ministra

Our father learned this from his mother who would make it for him on winter afternoons (adding lots of garlic and chilli) as a quick and warming snack. It's called ministra in Hebrew but it's more of a tomato broth with pasta and potatoes than minestrone. We've even started serving it sprinkled with parmesan which makes it super-delicious.

- 3 tbsp vegetable oil
- 1 bulb garlic
- 1 tbsp tomato paste
- pinch cayenne pepper
- 1 tbsp paprika
- 3 large ripe tomatoes, roughly chopped
- 1 tsp salt
- 1 tbsp vegetable stock powder
- 410 g tinned chopped tomatoes
- 1 tbsp sugar
- 500 g Nicola potatoes, cubed
- 150 g penne pasta
- 2 litres water

Slice the garlic cloves into thickish slices. Fry the garlic in oil on a low heat in a pot. Add the tomato paste, cayenne pepper and paprika and mix through. Allow a layer of sediment to appear before adding the rest of the ingredients, excluding the potatoes and pasta. Simmer the liquid for 30 – 40 minutes until all the flavours have come together. About half an hour before you are ready to eat, add the potatoes and simmer for about 10 minutes. Then finally add the pasta and cook through until al dente and serve.

Serves 6

Cook's Note
If left to stand for too long the pasta will absorb all the liquid, so the ministra must be served as soon as the pasta is cooked.

Tomato Soup

We've got our everyday soups at Sababa and then we've got our 'special soups', which are more concentrated. This is definitely 'special' because it takes a lot of tomatoes but only makes a small quantity. Roasting the tomatoes maximises their sweetness and the soup is delicious served with a fresh basil purée and toasted ciabatta.

- 1 kg Rosa tomatoes
- 1 kg Roma tomatoes
- 2 red peppers, cut into chunks
- 3 onions, quartered
- 1 red chilli, sliced (optional)
- 1 garlic, peeled (the whole bulb)
- 1 cup extra virgin olive oil
- 1 tbsp vegetable stock
- 3 tsp sugar
- salt and freshly ground black pepper to taste

Preheat the oven to 180°C.

Mix the tomatoes, peppers, onions, chilli and garlic with the olive oil and pinch of salt and pepper. Transfer it all to a baking tray and roast the vegetables in the oven for about 40 minutes until they go soft and lightly browned.

Then transfer it all to a pot and add 1 litre of water, the vegetable stock, sugar, salt and pinch of black pepper. Bring the soup to the boil and then continue cooking on a low heat for another half an hour. Blend the soup until smooth and then check the seasoning.

Serves 6 - 8

Cook's Note
The riper the tomatoes are, the better the soup will taste.

Mushroom Soup

Another one of our 'special soups' which we only make for special occasions or to order.

- 60 ml vegetable oil
- 2 onions, diced
- 1 tsp salt
- pinch of freshly ground black pepper to taste
- 1 kg button mushrooms, sliced
- 3 tbsp vegetable stock powder
- 1 tbsp fresh thyme, chopped
- 1½ litres water
- 250 ml cream

Sauté the onions with the vegetable oil, salt and pepper in a pot until they soften.

Add the mushrooms and continue cooking until the mushrooms brown slightly.

Add the stock, thyme and water and gently simmer the soup for 30 – 40 minutes.

Finally add the cream and simmer for another 10 minutes.

Serves 6 – 8

Pea and Mint Soup

We don't serve a lot of cold soups at Sababa but quite a lot of people want soup for dinner parties in summer. In this recipe the yoghurt and mint have a cooling effect.

- 2 tbsp sunflower oil
- 70 g onion, diced
- 70 g carrot, chopped
- 1 clove garlic, crushed
- pinch of salt and freshly ground black pepper to taste
- 500 g frozen peas
- 1 tsp vegetable stock powder
- 750 ml water
- 20 g mint, chopped
- 100 ml Greek yoghurt
- squeeze of lemon

Fry the onions and carrots together in the oil until they soften. Add the garlic, peas, salt and pepper and mix through for a minute. Then add the stock and water and simmer for 10 minutes. Remove the pot from the heat and blend the soup with the mint, yoghurt and lemon juice.

Serve the soup hot or cold with a dollop of yoghurt.

Serves 4

Cook's Note
To retain the bright green colour of the peas, make sure the soup doesn't boil for more than 10 minutes.

Minestrone Soup

My dad makes ministra and my mom makes this more conventional minestrone that is packed with veggies.

- half a bunch of celery, sliced
- 1 onion, diced
- 100 g potatoes, cubed
- 100 g sweet potato, cubed
- 100 g carrots, cubed
- 100 g green beans, chopped
- 1 small green cabbage, shredded
- 100 g baby marrow, cubed
- 200 g haricot beans, soaked overnight in 3 times the quantity of water
- 820 g chopped tomatoes
- 200 g tomato paste
- 3 tbsp vegetable stock
- 3 ½ litres water
- 2 tsp salt
- 2 ½ ml freshly ground black pepper
- 2 tbsp sugar
- pinch of salt and freshly ground black pepper to taste

Place all the ingredients together in a pot and boil on a medium heat for about an hour. Check the seasoning and add more salt, pepper or sugar as required.

Serves 6 – 8

Spicy Butternut Soup

This spicy Moroccan soup with cumin, chilli and ginger has an unusual kick – not your average sweet butternut soup.

- 2 tbsp vegetable oil
- 2 onions, diced
- 2 cloves garlic, crushed
- 5 cm chunk of ginger, roughly chopped
- 1 red chilli (optional)
- 1 tsp salt
- pinch of freshly ground black pepper
- 1 tbsp turmeric
- 1 tsp cayenne pepper
- 1 tbsp cumin
- 1 kg butternut, cut into chunks
- 100 g carrot, cut into chunks
- 250 g sweet potato, cut into chunks
- 1 bunch celery (stalks only), sliced
- 2 tbsp stock

Fry the onions in oil until soft and translucent. Add the garlic, ginger and chilli and stir. Add the spices and mix through for a few minutes. Add the rest of the ingredients to the pot and just enough water to cover all the vegetables. Bring to the boil and then continue cooking on a low heat for about an hour. Add a little more water if the soup is looking too thick.

Use a hand blender to blend all the ingredients together until thick and smooth. Check the seasoning for salt and pepper.

Serves 6 - 8

LUNCH BOX SPECIAL

(Choose 1 main & 3 Salads!!) *

	Medium	Large
• CHICKEN/VEG	-R50	-R60
• BEEF/LAMB	-R55	-R65
• FILLET	-R65	-R75

TODAY'S SPECIALS

BLACK PEPPER FILLET
TURKISH BEEF CASSEROLE
LAMB KOFTES
CHICKEN KOFTES
CHICKEN SCHNITZEL
CHICKEN & PRUNES CASSEROL
HERBY CHICKEN
CAJUN CHICKEN
LEEK & BEEF STEW
FISHCAKES
VEGETABLE LASAGNE
SALMON FILLET

FISH

'Chraime is symbolic of Friday afternoons in Israel, getting together with our dad's mom, Toni, and the other family members who live there. We all love chraime and each person has their turn to be served, waiting patiently for my gran to offer up their portion lovingly with her time-worn hands.' – Nirit

Chraime

Chraime is, without a doubt, a special-occasion dish. It's red, it's hot, there's a hint of sweetness from the slowly sautéed onions and at the same time it's spicy. Everyone in my family has their own version of chraime – our aunt's is more saucy; our gran's is stronger – and I don't know if it's because our mom's chraime was what we ate growing up, but for me hers is the best! On Friday nights we have it with kitka bread for dunking in the sauce – the best way to eat it – on Passover (when there's no kitka) it's never as good.

- 1 onion, finely diced
- 2 tbsp vegetable oil
- 1 garlic, crushed (the whole bulb)
- 2 tbsp lemon juice
- 2 ml chilli powder or 1 red chilli, chopped
- 2 tbsp sweet paprika
- 130 g tomato paste
- 500 ml water
- 1 tsp sugar
- 2 ml cumin, ground
- 1 kg salmon or yellowtail, filleted and skin off

Fry the onion in oil until soft and translucent. Mix the garlic, lemon juice, chilli and paprika together and then add it to the onions in the pan. Add the tomato paste and cook for another few minutes. Add the water and sugar and cook the sauce for about 15 minutes so that all the flavours come together.

Cut the salmon into 150 g pieces and cook them in the sauce for about 10 minutes until the fish is just cooked through. Turn the heat off and sprinkle with the cumin.

Serve the fish warm or at room temperature with some extra sauce and chunky white bread.

Serves 6 - 8

Cook's Note
Chraime is best made with a firmer fish. We always used yellowtail but to make it extra special you could use Norwegian salmon. For improved flavour, soak the fish in lemon juice overnight.

Fish Cakes with Lemon and Parsley Aioli

The Ashkenazis love fish, so we came up with this recipe when we opened our first shop and added our Sababa touch: A little spice, a lot of fresh herbs, and – something we also add when making meatballs or burger patties – some grated onion and carrot fried off in oil to lend a richer flavour.

- 1 tbsp sunflower oil
- 1 onion, finely diced
- 1 carrot, grated
- 500 g hake
- 2 cloves garlic, crushed
- 2 eggs
- 30 g Italian flat-leaf parsley, chopped
- zest of 1 lemon
- 50 ml fresh lemon juice
- pinch of salt and freshly ground black pepper to taste
- oil for frying

AIOLI
- 100 g mayonnaise
- half tsp crushed garlic
- 1 tbsp fresh lemon juice
- 1 tbsp Italian flat-leaf parsley, finely chopped
- 1 tbsp extra virgin olive oil
- pinch of salt and freshly ground black pepper to taste

Fry the onions and carrots with the sunflower oil until soft. Blend the hake in a food processor until it just breaks up. Once the onion mixture has cooled down, combine the fish together with the onion mixture and add the garlic, eggs, parsley, lemon zest, lemon juice, salt and pepper.

Heat a non-stick pan with a little oil. Shape the fishcakes into 5 cm round shapes and fry the fishcakes for a few minutes on each side until the fish is cooked through and golden brown.

For the aioli, simply combine all the ingredients together.

Serves 4 – 5

Fish Pie

Sababa offers a selection of pies, baked goods and lasagnes that change daily and we chose this particular fish pie because it's classic and easy to make. We've also included all kinds of vegetables, so it's got everything in one dish. With all our pies, I find finishing them with a sprinkling of sesame seeds adds a nice nuttiness – and it reminds us of home.

- 1.3 kg Norwegian salmon, filleted with skin off
- 2 tbsp olive oil
- handful of dill, chopped
- pinch of salt and freshly ground black pepper to taste
- 2 red onions, diced
- 150 g carrots, diced
- 150 g green beans, chopped
- 2 tbsp olive oil
- 400 g puff pastry
- 1 egg yolk
- 2 tbsp sesame seeds

BÉCHAMEL SAUCE
- 100 g butter
- 100 g flour
- 1 litre milk
- 1 tsp salt
- pinch of salt and freshly ground black pepper to taste

Prepare the salmon by rubbing it with the olive oil, dill, salt and pepper. Let the salmon marinade for about an hour in the fridge and then grill it in the oven on 200°C for 20 - 30 minutes.

Prepare the béchamel by melting the butter in a pot. Add the flour all at once and stir until it comes together. Add the milk, salt and pepper and on a low heat keep whisking the mixture until it thickens.

In the meantime pan fry the onions, carrots and green beans in olive oil with salt and pepper. Once the salmon has cooled slightly, break it up and mix it together with the vegetables and béchamel.

Preheat the oven to 170°C. Transfer the mixture to an ovenproof dish and place a layer of rolled out puff pastry to cover the dish. Brush the pastry with egg yolk and sprinkle with sesame seeds. Bake the pie in the oven for about half an hour until the pastry is golden brown and cooked through.

Serves 10 - 12

Fried Fish with Tomato and Cumin Sauce

Our version of fried fish is a crumbed line fish. We try to avoid too much frying at Sababa because we've got a reputation for healthy food, but when we do it, it's a big hit. I think fried fish works best with hake – it's soft and light and we have so much good-quality hake available in South Africa.

- 1.2 kg filleted hake with skin off
- 4 eggs
- 1 tsp garlic, crushed
- 1 tbsp hot English mustard
- 500 ml breadcrumbs
- 1 tbsp paprika
- 1 tbsp cayenne pepper
- 1 tbsp dried origanum
- pinch of salt and freshly ground black pepper to taste

SAUCE
- 2 tbsp vegetable oil
- 2 onions, diced
- pinch of salt and freshly ground black pepper to taste
- 2 ml cumin
- 2 ml paprika
- 1 tsp sugar
- 1 tbsp tomato paste
- 500 g Rosa tomatoes, quartered
- 180 ml water
- 2 tbsp extra virgin olive oil

Portion the hake according to the size you would like to serve it. Whisk together the eggs, garlic and mustard and pour over the fish. Leave the fish in the fridge to marinate overnight.

The next day prepare your breadcrumb mixture by combining the breadcrumbs with the paprika, cayenne pepper, dried origanum, salt and pepper.

Heat the oil in a frying pan and when the correct temperature is reached, cover the hake portions one at a time in the breadcrumbs. Fry the fish in batches until it is crisp and cooked through.

To make the sauce, fry the onions in the vegetable oil. Add the salt, pepper, cumin and paprika, and mix through. Then add the tomato paste and fresh tomatoes.

Stir this mixture for a minute and then add the water. Cook the sauce on a medium heat until the tomatoes have broken down and the sauce has thickened. Blend the sauce together with the olive oil.

Serve the fish with the tomato and cumin sauce and some freshly cut potato fries.

Serves 6 - 8

Cook's Note
Sesame seeds can be added to the crumb mixture, as seen in the recipe for chicken schnitzel.

MEAT & CHICKEN

A note on paprika

In Israel people shop at markets, or at least at specialist suppliers on a day-to-day basis. Every suburb has some vegetable shops, bakeries and butcheries – and spice shops. Here the spices are ground to order and the paprika is so fresh it is still wet when you buy it. Each time my parents go to Israel I put together a list of things for them to bring back. It's usually food items and the list will always include: za'atar, sumac and paprika. There's such a big difference between the paprika you buy there and what you find on a supermarket shelf in South Africa. Even the colour sets it apart – it's bright, bright red. We've taken into account that you may only have access to standard-issue paprika – sometimes that's all we can get too – so these recipes will turn out no less delicious. But if you do have a friend or relative who is travelling to a place where top-quality, freshly-ground paprika is available, ask them to bring you some – it will take your cooking to another level.

Paprika and Garlic Roast Chicken

This recipe came from our maternal grandmother. It uses a lot of garlic and a lot of paprika and it is the simplest chicken dish you can make. At home we all like our chicken very well cooked – and if there's skin, it must be crisp – but this is a family preference. I don't mind if the meat is slightly dry as a result because we always have it with a sauce, like tahina, as it would be eaten in Israel. This is delicious as a sandwich filler but there are seldom leftovers because it is one of those dishes that everybody loves – and can't get enough of!

- 24 chicken pieces (drumsticks and thighs are best for this recipe)
- 250 ml canola oil
- 5 tbsp paprika
- 1 tbsp chicken spice
- 2 ml mustard powder
- 1 garlic, peeled (the whole bulb)
- 2 tsp salt
- pinch of freshly ground black pepper

Preheat the oven to 180°C.

Crush all the garlic and then mix it together with the oil, paprika, chicken spice, mustard powder, salt and pepper. Brush the paste onto the chicken pieces, coating them well. Roast the chicken in the oven for about 45 minutes until the skin is crispy and the chicken is cooked through.

Serves 10 - 12

Cook's Note

We like to use mostly brown meat (legs and thighs), leaving it on the bone. Because the darker meat is more succulent, it lends itself to a longer cooking time. If you prefer chicken breasts, those with skin on and still on the bone are also better suited to this recipe.

Stuffed Cabbage Rolls with Mince and Rice

In Israel, my grandparents cook a wide variety of stuffed vegetables: stuffed onions, stuffed baby marrows, stuffed aubergines, and stuffed tomatoes. My mother prefers to stuff cabbage leaves and peppers, because the peppers in this country are a good size for filling. Some people poach stuffed cabbage leaves in stock but with our Italian-influenced Libyan background we simmer them in a tomato sauce. The preparation is quite time-consuming so it's not suitable for everyday cooking – instead we save this for Sabbath dinners.

- 1 green cabbage
- 500 g beef mince
- 1 handful Italian flat-leaf parsley, finely chopped
- 2 onions, finely chopped
- 1 egg
- pinch of salt and freshly ground black pepper to taste
- 80 ml vegetable oil
- 1 tsp turmeric
- 1 tsp paprika
- 1 cup basmati rice
- 125 ml water

SAUCE
- 90 g tomato paste
- 1 tsp sugar
- 1 tsp salt
- pinch of freshly ground black pepper
- 1 lemon, juiced
- 750 ml water
- 400 g tinned, chopped tomatoes
- 1 handful Italian flat-leaf parsley, finely chopped

Clean the cabbage and remove the core with a sharp knife. Put the cabbage in a pot filled with water and bring the water to the boil with the pot lid on. Allow the water to boil for 10 minutes and then turn the heat off and leave the cabbage to soak in the water for an hour.

Prepare the filling by mixing together the beef mince with the parsley, 1 onion, egg, and the salt and freshly ground black pepper.

Heat the oil in a frying pan and fry the rest of the chopped onion until it softens. Then add the spices, salt and pepper, and mix through for a minute. Add the rice, and then finally the water. Keep stirring until the all the water has been absorbed. Once the rice mixture has cooled down completely, add it to the beef mixture and combine the two together well.
After an hour remove the cabbage from the pot, drain and separate all the leaves. Place a spoonful of the mixture on each leaf and roll them up to make parcels, tucking the sides in so that mixture can't ooze out. Once you have used up all the cabbage leaves and filling, place the parcels closely together in a shallow pot.

Prepare the sauce by combining all the ingredients, except for the parsley. Pour the sauce over the cabbage rolls and place a heavy plate on top of the parcels to keep them from opening up during the cooking process. Bring the sauce to the boil and then continue cooking on a low heat for about an hour. Just before serving sprinkle with the finely chopped parsley.

Makes about 15 cabbage parcels

Sweet Sticky Chicken

This isn't an Israeli dish at all; it's something my mother learned in South Africa after enjoying it at a dinner party one night. We eat it every year on the night before the big fast, Yom Kippur (Jewish Day of Atonement).

- 125 ml strong chutney
- 125 ml mayonnaise
- 150 ml water
- 10 pcs skinless chicken (thighs and legs)
- 1 tbsp chicken stock
- 45 g brown onion soup powder
- 55 g dried onion flakes
- 2 ml paprika
- 2 ml nutmeg
- 2 ml chilli powder
- 1 ml cinnamon
- pinch of salt and freshly
- ground black pepper to taste

Preheat the oven to 180°C.

Combine the chutney, mayonnaise, water, stock and brown onion soup powder. Rub the chicken pieces with all the spices and then pour the marinade mover the pieces, making sure all the pieces are well-coated. Roast the chicken in the oven for about 40 – 50 minutes until the chicken is cooked through and golden brown.

Serves 5 - 6

Lamb Koftes

At Sababa we incorporate lots of chopped, soft herbs into our koftas, like mint, coriander, parsley and dill. We also like to cook our koftas in a pan so that they develop a crisp, nicely browned exterior. You could do the same or pan fry to get a good colour and then pop them in the oven to finish off the cooking. Sometimes we cook them like meatballs, in a tomato sauce, and they're great with tahina on the side. We've even made Mediterranean burgers as canapés by slipping a kofta into a bun.

- 1 kg lamb mince
- 40 g Italian flat-leaf parsley, chopped finely
- 40 g coriander, chopped finely
- 2 onions, finely diced
- 1 tsp paprika
- 1 tsp cumin
- 2 ml cinnamon
- pinch of salt and freshly ground black pepper to taste
- 1 cup pine nuts, toasted
- 2 eggs
- oil for frying

Combine all the ingredients together in a bowl and mix well.

Heat a little oil in a frying pan and pan fry golf-size balls of the mixture for about 1 minute on each side to give them some colour.

About half an hour before you are ready to serve the koftes, preheat the oven to 180°C and finish the koftes in the oven for about 10 minutes until they are hot and cooked through.

Serves 8 – 10

Cook's Note
At Sababa we offer many different koftas: lamb, chicken, beef, sometimes even turkey. To make beef or chicken koftas substitute the same quantity of minced beef or chicken for the minced lamb. Serve with some tahina sauce on the side.

Chicken and Haricot Bean Stew

This is my personal recipe, but very much in the Libyan tradition of slow-cooking and one-pot meals. In winter we make many stews using different combinations of vegetables and this is an example of one of them.

- 2 onions, diced
- 125 ml sunflower oil
- 1.2 kg chicken breasts cut into strips
- 115 g tomato paste
- pinch of salt and freshly ground black pepper to taste
- 10 ml turmeric
- 20 ml paprika
- 5 ml cumin
- 2 ml cinnamon
- 2 tbsp chicken stock
- 2 litres water
- 600 g green beans, halved
- 500 g haricot beans
- 500 g baby marrows, peeled and halved

Soak the haricot beans overnight in three times the amount of water.

In a large shallow pot, fry the onions until soft and golden brown. Add the chicken strips and continue frying until the chicken is golden on the outside. Add the tomato paste and continue cooking for 2 minutes. Then add the salt, pepper, turmeric, paprika, cumin, cinnamon and stock. Lastly add the water and then the green beans, haricot beans and the baby marrow. Bring the stew to the boil and then simmer for about an hour until all the vegetables and chicken are soft and the sauce has reduced slightly. Adjust the seasoning if necessary.

Serves 10 – 12

Rare Roast Beef Fillet

Fillet is a favourite in both Sababa stores and what makes ours a little bit extra-delicious is the overnight marinating. It is very simple to cook, but you do need to plan ahead.

- 1½ – 2 kg beef fillet
- 10 g thyme, chopped
- 10 g rosemary
- 4 cloves garlic, crushed
- zest and juice of 1 lemon
- freshly ground black pepper to taste
- 125 ml olive oil
- 125 ml soy sauce
- pinch of salt

Marinate the fillet overnight with the chopped thyme, rosemary, garlic, zest and juice of the lemon, black pepper, olive oil and soy sauce, making sure the fillet is well-covered with the marinade.

Preheat the oven to 200°C and bring the fillet to room temperature before roasting. Once the oven is hot, salt the fillet and roast in the oven for about 20 minutes. Allow the fillet to rest for at least 15 minutes before slicing or all the juices from the meat will run out and you will be left with dry beef. Once the fillet is sliced, pour the cooked sauce over the meat and serve.

Serves 8 – 10

Cook's Note
If you prefer your meat medium or well-done you can either cook it in the oven for an extra 20 – 30 minutes whole, or even after it has been sliced. The meat can be served hot or cold.

Lamb Knuckle Stew

We learned this recipe from my mom, who in turn had learned it from her South African friends, but made it her own by adding her signature spicing. The meat literally falls off the bone and the way we would serve it at home is with couscous and tirshi. The tirshi is very lemony and very garlicky so as you can imagine – in the same way a lot of people serve gremolata with lamb – it all works beautifully together.

- 2 kg sliced lamb knuckle
- 3 carrots, cut into chunks
- 2 onions, quartered
- 1 garlic, peeled (the whole bulb)
- 120 g tomato paste
- 1 tsp cinnamon
- 2 tsp cumin
- 4 tsp paprika
- 2 tsp sugar
- 2 tsp salt
- 1 tsp freshly ground black pepper
- 1 litre water

Place the lamb, carrots, onions and garlic in a shallow pot. Combine the rest of the ingredients in a mixing bowl and then pour over the lamb. Bring to the boil and then gently simmer until the lamb is soft and falls off the bone easily. This should take about 3 hours.

Serves 6 – 8

Lemon and Herb Grilled Chicken

At home we always had pita breads in the freezer and tahina paste in our pantry. For a quick meal we would make a piece of grilled chicken and a fresh salad, adding toasted pitas and tahina sauce. We have found that South Africans like lemon and herb grilled chicken and at Sababa we cook it on a griddle pan, which achieves a nicely charred outside, leaving the chicken tender inside. It's a healthy, light lunch and here we have combined it with baba ganoush.

- 1.2 kg chicken breast, skinless and boneless
- 3 lemons
- handful Italian flat-leaf parsley
- handful of basil
- 2 cloves of garlic
- 125 ml olive oil
- pinch of salt and freshly ground black pepper to taste

Cut the chicken breasts in half widthways to make 2 thinner pieces.

Grate the zest of the lemons and squeeze all the juice out. With a hand blender, blend together the herbs with the garlic, olive oil, a pinch of freshly ground black pepper, half the lemon juice and all the lemon zest. Pour the marinade over the chicken and leave it to marinate in the fridge for at least 1 hour.

Once you are ready to cook the chicken, heat a griddle pan on the stove top. Sprinkle some salt over the chicken pieces and then grill them on the hot griddle pan for a few minutes on each side until they have a nice charred colour and the chicken is cooked all the way through. Once you have cooked all the chicken, pour the remaining lemon over the chicken and serve.

Serves 6 – 8

Cook's Note
Serve the chicken with tahina sauce or baba ganoush.

Moroccan Roast Brisket

I don't think my mother has ever cooked brisket and I know that my paternal grandparents have definitely never cooked it. Aside from it being very much an Ashkenazi tradition, it's usually sweetish and our family palate is more savoury. We decided to try it out and made our sauce sweet but also spicy, adding za'atar and cinnamon to take it in a Moroccan direction. The tomato-onion sauce is a nod to our Libyan roots and because we live in South Africa we added a dash of chutney!

- 125 ml extra virgin olive oil
- 1 tsp paprika
- 2 tsp cumin
- 1 tsp cinnamon
- 2 tsp za'atar
- 2 tbsp vegetable oil
- 2½ – 3 kg brisket
- 1 tsp salt
- 2 ml freshly ground black pepper
- 3 onions, sliced
- 400 g Rosa tomatoes, halved
- 820 g chopped tomatoes
- 5 cloves garlic, halved
- 55 g brown onion soup
- 1 cup chutney
- 2 cups water

Mix the olive oil with the paprika, cumin, cinnamon and za'atar. Rub the brisket with the spicy marinade and leave in the fridge for at least an hour.

Heat the vegetable oil in a pan, season the meat with salt and pepper and then seal it in the pan until the meat is browned. Keep the brisket aside and cook the onions in the same pan until they soften.

Preheat the oven to 170°C.

Combine the rest of the ingredients together in a mixing bowl. Put the brisket in a deep roasting pan together with the onions and the sauce. Cover the dish with foil and roast for about 3 hours until the brisket is very soft. For the last half an hour you can roast the brisket without the foil.

If you want to thinly slice the brisket, you will need to cool the brisket completely before slicing. Alternatively, simply pull the meat apart and serve.

Serves 8 – 10

Dad's Weber Smoked Chicken

Although this isn't something we could ever make at Sababa we had to include it because so many South Africans own a Weber braai. My dad doesn't add anything out of the ordinary but it's his cooking method that's important. He leaves the chicken on the braai for hours so that smokiness flavours the meat, which just falls apart in your mouth. It really is a brilliant recipe.

- 1 whole free range chicken

STUFFING
- 4 cloves of garlic
- half an onion
- half a lemon
- 2 sprigs of rosemary
- 2 sprigs of thyme

MARINADE
- 125 ml white wine
- 1 ml mustard seeds
- 1 ml coriander seeds
- 1 ml freshly ground black pepper
- 2 ml salt
- 1 tbsp sweet paprika
- 1 tbsp chicken spice
- juice of 1 lemon
- 80 ml extra virgin olive oil

Mix all the ingredients for the marinade together and rub all over the chicken with your hands, making sure that every part of the chicken is covered. Then fill the cavity of the chicken with the stuffing ingredients, cover the chicken and leave it in the fridge to marinate overnight.

The next day, take the chicken out of the fridge and prepare the fire in the Weber. Cook the chicken in an open foil container on a medium heat for 4 - 6 hours, checking every now and then that the temperature is correct and continually basting the chicken with the juices that are released.

Serves 4 - 6

Spicy Chicken Livers

When we were young my parents would throw big New Year's Eve parties. The Hebrew calendar starts in September with the high holy festival Rosh Hashanah, but because all the South Africans were celebrating New Year in January, my parents would invite their Israeli friends over on that evening. There would always be loud music, they would always braai, and the starter was always chicken livers cooked on one of those big, flat griddle pans with lots and lots and lots of onions. My parents and I agree: the more onions the better. Where we differ is I like my chicken livers more saucy whereas they like them hot and quite dry.

- 3 onions, sliced
- 80 ml vegetable oil
- 500 g chicken livers
- 2 ml chilli powder
- 2 ml smoked paprika
- 2 ml ground cumin
- 60 ml brandy
- 125 ml cream
- pinch of salt and freshly ground black pepper to taste

Sauté the onions with 60 ml of vegetable oil and a pinch of salt and pepper until the onions soften and go a dark brown colour. This will take 10 - 15 minutes and you will need to stir every so often so that the onions don't burn. Remove the onions and in the same pan heat the remaining oil and pan fry the livers for a few minutes together with the rest of the spices and a pinch of salt and pepper. Add the brandy and continue cooking until it has all been absorbed. Finally add the cream and onions, and reduce the sauce slightly. Serve the livers hot with white bread.

Serves 4

How to make breadcrumps

We make our own breadcrumbs because there are always leftover pitas, whether it's from falafel night or the market, so that way nothing goes to waste. We break up the bread and dry it out in the oven at 120°C for a couple of hours. Then we crush the toasted pitas – but never until the crumbs are completely fine – we leave a few chunky bits to give more texture. Sometimes we make the crumbs at the end of the day and just switch off the oven, leaving the pitas to dry out overnight. Or we might toast the pitas, first at 170°C and after 10 minutes bring the temperature down to 120°C to dry them out.

Sesame Crumbed Chicken Schnitzel

In Israel schnitzel is hugely popular – especially in a sandwich – and we grew up eating schnitzel at least once a week. My mother's personal touch is to add spice and sesame seeds (sesame seeds are big in our home) and she taught us, as did our family in Israel, that it's best to marinate the chicken in egg, garlic and mustard overnight. That way the flavours permeate the chicken breast and you can take it straight from the egg and into the crumbs before frying. For Passover we do a version with matzo meal and I almost prefer it to the breadcrumbs. In fact, one customer told me it looks just like KFC (meaning it as a compliment!) but for Passover we don't use the sesame seeds, because although the Sephardim eat them over Passover, Ashkenazis do not.

- 800 g chicken breast, skinless and boneless
- 3 eggs
- 1 tsp garlic, crushed
- 1 tbsp hot English mustard
- 500 ml breadcrumbs
- 125 ml sesame seeds
- 1 tbsp paprika
- 2 ml cayenne pepper
- 1 tbsp dried origanum
- pinch of salt and freshly ground black pepper to taste
- oil for frying

Prepare the chicken breasts by halving them widthways to make them thinner. Combine the eggs, garlic and mustard in a bowl and pour over the chicken. Marinate the chicken overnight for the best results.

Prepare the breadcrumb mixture by combining the breadcrumbs with the sesame seeds, paprika, cayenne pepper, dried origanum and the salt and pepper.

When you are ready to start frying, heat the oil in a pan and coat the chicken well with the sesame-crumb mixture. Fry the chicken for a few minutes on each side until the chicken is crispy, golden on the outside, and cooked through on the inside.

Serves 4 – 6

Cook's Note
The schnitzels can be served hot or at room temperature and make great sandwiches.

Mafrum

Mafrum is deeply Libyan in origin. We serve it with couscous and tirshi and because it is so time-consuming to make, mafrum is a treat generally reserved for the Sabbath and Jewish festivals. It is extremely satisfying and very welcome over Passover when bread and couscous are not allowed and everyone complains they eat so much but remain permanently hungry! When making it for Passover we substitute matzo meal for the flour and, even though Sephardim may have rice over this time, serve the mafrum without a carbohydrate accompaniment.

- 7 large potatoes
- 300 g breadcrumbs or matzo meal
- 4 – 6 eggs, whisked
- vegetable oil for frying

FILLING
- 500 g beef mince
- 2 eggs, beaten
- 2 tbsp breadcrumbs or matzo meal
- 1 onion, chopped
- 5 cloves garlic, crushed
- 30 g coriander, chopped
- 30 g Italian flat-leaf parsley, chopped
- 1 tsp salt
- 1 ml freshly ground black pepper
- 1 ml cayenne pepper
- 1 tbsp paprika
- pinch of nutmeg
- pinch of cinnamon

SAUCE
- 1 onion, sliced
- 5 cloves of garlic, sliced thinly
- 130 g tomato paste
- 1 tsp paprika
- pinch of salt and freshly ground black pepper to taste
- 2 cups water

'The spice in the meat parcels blends with the tomato sauce so beautifully I usually cannot wait for lunch the next day to eat the leftovers!' – Nirit

Peel and slice each potato into 3 lengthways. Sprinkle the potatoes with salt and leave them to rest for an hour. After an hour rinse them and then slice again lengthways but only going half way – at this point if you open up the potato slice where it is cut, it forms a pocket.

For the filling, simply combine all the ingredients together in a mixing bowl. Fill each potato pocket with the mince filling.

Heat some vegetable oil in a frying pan and have 2 bowls on the side: one with the breadcrumbs or matzo meal and one with the eggs. When the oil is hot, coat each potato pocket with the crumbs and then the egg. Fry them in oil so that each of the sides goes golden brown. Once all the potato pockets are fried, place them in a shallow pot, slightly overlapping, and making sure they are packed tightly together.

Combine all the ingredients for the sauce together and pour over the potato pockets.

Add more water if necessary to just cover the potato pockets. Bring the pot to the boil and then simmer slowly for about an hour.

Serves 10 – 12

Cook's Note
The fried potato pockets keep very well in the freezer so when you do decide to make them, make big batches. That way you can use however many you need, whenever you want to cook them, and most of your work is already done.

See recipe for couscous and tirshi on page 156

SALADS & VEGETABLES

Some of these salads were launched at Sababa, some I learned from my mom and some we came up with along the way – we experiment every day. The way a salad comes together in your mouth is so important and a lot of the time, what differentiates a good salad from a bad salad are the proportions of the vegetables. Take the time to shred your cabbage finely or chop your Israeli salad into perfectly uniform pieces, so you have the right ratio of ingredients in every bite.

Israeli Salad

Israeli salad is almost always part of our meals. The standard ingredients are: cucumber, tomato, parsley and onion, dressed with lemon juice and olive oil. Some people add spring onions, others add peppers and some add radish. We've added everything to ours because Sababa salads are always abundant, colourful and packed with ingredients.

- 400 g Israeli cucumbers, diced
- 4 small salad peppers, diced
- 400 g Rosa tomatoes, diced
- 4 radishes, sliced
- 1 red onion, diced
- 2 spring onions, thinly sliced
- 1 – 2 lemons, juiced
- 60 ml olive oil
- pinch of salt and freshly ground black pepper to taste
- handful of Italian flat-leaf parsley, chopped

Prepare all the vegetables. Just before you are ready to serve the salad, add the olive oil, lemon juice, salt, pepper and parsley. Toss and serve.

Serves 6 – 8

Cook's Note
Long English cucumbers can be quite watery so use the smaller Israeli or Mediterranean cucumbers, which have an earthy flavour and a crunchy texture. If you can't find Israeli cucumbers deseed the English cucumbers before using.

Rice Salad

I love rice but often when I'm offered rice it is plain boiled. The rice we ate at home was always more of a meal on its own and not just an accompaniment to something else. We grew up with Persian rice, which is made by frying sliced potatoes in a pan before adding rice and dill. As the rice cooks, the potatoes become crusty. Then you turn the whole pot upside down onto a plate so that you've got a mound of rice covered by a potato crust – it's amazing! Persian rice was the original inspiration for this recipe and the dill rice with peas that we serve at Sababa.

- 1 cup small brown lentils
- 125 ml vegetable oil
- 500 g jasmine rice
- 1 tbsp vegetable stock powder
- pinch of salt and freshly ground black pepper to taste
- 400 ml dried onion flakes
- 5 cups water
- 100 g carrots, diced
- 100 g green beans, diced
- 250 g frozen peas
- 1 handful dill, chopped
- 2 handfuls Italian flat-leaf parsley, chopped

Cook the lentils in 3 times the amount of water until they are just soft.

Heat the oil in a pot and add the rice. Mix through for a minute and then add the stock, salt, pepper and onion flakes. Add the water, vegetables and dill, and then cook the rice on a low heat until all the water has been absorbed. Turn the heat off and put a clean dry cloth over the pot with the lid over the cloth. Allow the rice to steam in this way for about 20 minutes. Mix the lentils into the rice and once the rice has cooled add the chopped parsley.

Serves 8 – 10

Barley and Roast Vegetable Salad with Lemon and Parsley

- 2 large aubergines
- extra virgin olive oil
- pinch of salt and freshly ground black pepper to taste
- 300 g beetroot
- 200 g carrots
- 200 g sweet potato
- 300 g baby marrow
- 200 g butternut
- 500 g barley
- 2 lemons, zest and juice
- 2 handfuls Italian flat-leaf parsley

Prepare the aubergines by cutting them into small cubes and salt them to remove the bitterness. Dry them after 10 minutes before roasting. Mix the aubergine with 50 ml of olive oil and a pinch of salt and pepper. Roast them in the oven until they are soft and slightly browned.

Prepare the beetroot, carrots, sweet potatoes, butternut and baby marrows by slicing them thinly.

You can cut them in whatever shape you think will look best in the dish. Mix each of these prepared vegetables with a tablespoon of olive oil and a pinch of salt and pepper, and roast each variety individually on trays until they are just cooked through.

In the meantime boil the barley in water until soft and cooked.

Once the barley has cooled down, mix it through with the lemon zest and juice, half of the finely chopped parsley and half of the assorted vegetables. Check the seasoning at this stage and adjust it with more salt and pepper if necessary.

Plate the salad onto your platter and finish it off with the rest of the vegetables. Drizzle with some more olive oil.

Serves 8 – 10

Cabbage Salad

This is a salad that can be eaten immediately, but the flavour will improve if you have the time to leave it for a couple of hours before serving. The best way to make it is to shred fresh cabbage as finely as you can – please don't use those packets of pre-cut cabbage!

- 300 g green cabbage
- 300 g red cabbage
- 40 g dill, finely chopped
- 50 ml olive oil
- 50 ml balsamic vinegar
- pinch of salt and freshly ground black pepper to taste
- 65 g sesame seeds

Shred the cabbages finely and combine in a bowl. Add the rest of the ingredients and mix well.

Serves 6 – 8

Cook's Note
This salad keeps well if prepared in advance but the dressing will soften the cabbage slightly. If you prefer a crunchier salad, only toss everything together just before serving.

Egg Salad

This is good together with a green salad or an Israeli salad, or as part of a mezze. It is our mom's recipe and the secret is a LOT of dill. We use dill in most things and often customers come into the shop and say, 'Ah! Dill again? You use dill in everything!' Even the staff ask, 'More dill?' It's just something we've been brought up with and I absolutely love the flavour.

- 20 large eggs
- 20 g dill, finely chopped
- 1 red onion, finely diced
- grated zest of 1 lemon (optional)
- pinch of salt and freshly ground black pepper

Boil the eggs for 8 minutes. Allow them to cool down completely. Then peel and grate them. Add the dill, red onion, lemon, salt and pepper, and mix through.

Serves 6 – 8

Roast Aubergine and Mixed Crunchy Greens Salad with Origanum Dressing

It's usually quite difficult to work with hardy herbs like fresh sage and origanum (for me they work best in slow cooking or bakes) but they work so well with the aubergines in this oreganum-sage vinaigrette.

- 1 kg aubergines
- 125 ml olive oil
- 180 g mangetout
- 180 g fine green beans
- 200 g fine asparagus
- pinch of salt and freshly ground black pepper to taste

DRESSING
- handful fresh sage
- handful fresh origanum
- 125 ml olive oil
- 80 ml red wine vinegar
- 2 cloves garlic, crushed
- pinch of salt and freshly ground black pepper to taste

Cook's Note

The American spelling for origanum is oregano. If fresh herbs are not available and dried herbs are used instead, please remember that the dried herbs are more concentrated and a little less should be used.

Preheat the oven to 180°C.

Cut the aubergines into medium-thickness wedges. Sprinkle salt over the aubergine wedges and after 10 minutes wash and pat them dry with kitchen paper. Put the wedges flat down onto the baking tray. Brush each wedge with olive oil and sprinkle with salt and pepper. Roast the aubergines in the oven until they are soft, browned and slightly crisp.

Prepare the greens but cutting them into the size you prefer. Bring a pot of water to the boil and add all the greens in at once. Blanche the greens by leaving them in the boiling water for a few minutes and then immediately run them under cold water.

Alternatively, once you take them out the boiling water, strain the greens through a colander and immediately put them into a bowl with ice and cold water. This process of blanching helps the vegetables stay crisp and crunchy for the salad and retain the colours.

Prepare the dressing by blending all the ingredients together with a hand blender.

Once you are ready to assemble the salad, first put the aubergine wedges down on a platter. Toss the greens in a mixing bowl with the dressing and then place them onto the wedges. Drizzle the remaining dressing over the salad.

Serves 8 – 10

Aubergine, Tahina and Tomato Salsa Salad

This salad is a meal in itself – all you need is a piece of fresh bread to scoop it all up.

- 1 kg aubergine
- half a red onion, chopped
- 300 g Rosa tomatoes, diced
- 20 g Italian flat-leaf parsley, chopped
- 20 g pine nuts, toasted
- olive oil for brushing
- freshly ground black pepper
- salt

DRESSING
- 3 tbsp tahina paste
- 2 tbsp water
- 1 lemon, juiced
- 1 clove garlic, crushed
- pinch of salt

Cook's Note
You could also char the aubergines whole over a flame and use only the fleshy insides.

Preheat the oven to 180°C.

Cut the aubergines into medium thickness wedges. Sprinkle salt over the aubergine wedges and after 10 minutes, wash and dry them. Put the wedges flat down onto the baking tray. Brush the wedges with olive oil and sprinkle with salt and black pepper.

Roast the aubergines in the oven until they are soft and slightly crisp. Once they are ready, leave them to cool.

Prepare the salsa by mixing together the chopped onion with the tomatoes and parsley.

For the dressing, simply whisk together the tahina paste with the lemon juice, garlic, water and salt. If it's too thick add a little more cold water, 1 tablespoon at a time, until the right consistency is reached.

Once you are ready to assemble the salad, place the wedges onto a flat platter. Pour the tahina dressing over the wedges and top with the tomato salsa and toasted pine nuts.

Serves 6 - 8

Tomato Salad

Whenever we were invited out to dinner and our mother was asked to make something, it was always this salad. It is a salad that I often go back to and it's always the first thing that pops into my head when putting a menu together. It is so straightforward that anyone interested in food could quite easily replicate it, but for some reason my mom has a special touch.

- 600 g Rosa tomatoes
- 100 g Calamata olives
- 60 g spring onions, sliced thinly
- 20 g dill
- 20 g pine nuts, toasted
- 2 tbsp extra virgin olive oil
- pinch of salt and freshly ground black pepper to taste

Cut the tomatoes in half and pit the olives. When you are ready to serve the salad combine all the ingredients together and mix well.

Serves 4 - 5

Cook's Note
Because the salad is so simple it relies on really good quality tomatoes and olives.

Beetroot and Nodini Salad

I love the look of cooked beets so we've had this recipe on the menu since day one.
Nodini is knotted mozzarella.

- 750 g beetroot
- 10 ml olive oil
- 10 ml red wine vinegar
- 1 clove garlic, crushed
- 10 ml honey
- pinch of salt and freshly ground black pepper to taste
- 40 g wild rocket
- 70 g carrots, peeled and cut into rounds
- 120 g fine green beans, blanched and halved
- 60 g nodini, torn into smaller pieces
- 15 g sunflower seeds, toasted

Roast the beetroot in foil at 180°C until they are just soft. Once they cool, peel and cut them into chunks.

Marinate the beetroot with olive oil, red wine vinegar, garlic, honey, salt and pepper.
To assemble the salad, place the rocket on a platter and cover it with the beetroot, green beans, carrots, nodini and sunflower seeds. Pour the remaining dressing from the beetroot over the salad and serve.

Serves 6

Cook's Note
We like to wrap our beetroot in foil before roasting. That way they stay sweeter. We find that beetroot loses a lot of flavour when boiled.

Chopped Mixed Green Salad

We use large quantities of fresh herbs in our salads. If I can say one thing about dressing a salad it is don't be shy with the herbs, especially in this salad.

- 90 g fine green beans
- 100 g fresh green peas
- 100 g sugar snaps, finely chopped
- 100 g mangetout, finely chopped
- 250 g corn kernels
- 1 red onion, sliced
- 10 g basil
- 10 g mint
- 125 ml Bulgarian yoghurt
- 2 tbsp olive oil
- pinch of salt and freshly ground black pepper to taste

Cut the fine green beans into 3 pieces. Combine the green beans, peas, sugar snaps, mangetout, corn kernels and red onion in a mixing bowl.

Prepare the dressing by blending the herbs with the yoghurt, olive oil, salt and pepper in a blender until the mixture is smooth. When you are ready to serve the salad, add the dressing to the vegetables and toss all the ingredients well together.

Serves 6 – 8

Raw Vegetable Salad

This salad is very healthy and you just know you're doing a good thing by eating it! Everything is chopped into pieces of approximately the same size, which is why the flavours come together so well.

- 500 g carrots
- 2 medium-sized broccoli heads
- 1 cauliflower
- 2 red onions
- 500 g baby marrows
- 40 g Italian flat-leaf parsley

DRESSING
- 50 ml red wine vinegar
- 100 ml olive oil
- 3 cloves of garlic, crushed
- pinch of salt and freshly ground black pepper to taste

Cut all the vegetables into the same size small blocks and chop the parsley finely.

For the dressing, mix all the ingredients together in a bowl. When you are ready to serve the salad, pour the dressing over the vegetables and toss well.

Serves 8 – 10

Broccoli, Cauliflower and Lentil Salad with Tahina Dressing

- 80 ml small brown lentils
- 400 g broccoli
- 400 g cauliflower
- 70 ml extra virgin olive oil
- 200 g Rosa tomatoes
- 15 g sunflower seeds, toasted
- 40 g wild rocket
- pinch of salt and freshly ground black pepper to taste

DRESSING
- 1 clove garlic, crushed
- 1 lemon, juiced
- 125 ml tahina paste
- 80 – 100 ml water
- pinch of salt

Cook the lentils in 3 times the mount of water until they are just soft. Strain off the water and allow them to cool slightly while preparing the rest of the elements.

Prepare the tahina dressing by whisking all the ingredients together until smooth. Keep the dressing aside in the fridge until you are ready to use it.

Preheat the oven to 180°C.

Roast the broccoli and cauliflower with 60 ml of olive oil and a pinch of salt and pepper for about 15 – 20 minutes, until the vegetables are golden and crisp.

Toss the tomatoes with the remainder of the olive oil and a pinch of salt and pepper and roast them in the oven on a tray until they soften and get slightly browned.

Once the cauliflower and broccoli are baked, combine them with the tahina dressing while they are still hot so that they readily absorb the flavour from the dressing.

When you are ready to serve the salad, assemble it by placing the rocket, broccoli and cauliflower on a platter and placing the roasted tomatoes, lentils and sunflower seeds above them.

Serves 6 – 8

Lentil Salad

- 250 g small brown lentils
- 1 cucumber, cubed
- 2 red peppers, cubed
- 2 yellow peppers, cubed
- 1 red onion, sliced
- 1 lemon, zest and juice
- 50 g Italian flat-leaf parsley, chopped
- 100 ml olive oil
- pinch of salt and freshly ground black pepper to taste

Cook the lentils in 3 times the amount of water until they are just cooked. Be careful not to overcook the lentils as they will taste chalky.

Once they have cooled down completely, add the rest of the ingredients. Mix everything together well and serve.

Serves 4

Roast Mushroom and Pepper Salad

This is served as part of the breakfast spread at our Bree Street restaurant in Cape Town.

- 250 g portabellini mushrooms
- 250 g brown mushrooms
- 250 g button mushrooms
- 2 red onions, cut into chunks
- 1 red pepper, sliced
- 1 yellow pepper, sliced
- 4 – 5 sprigs of thyme, chopped
- 100 ml olive oil
- pinch of salt and freshly ground black pepper to taste

Preheat the oven to 190°C.

Chop the mushrooms so that they are all similar in size. Mix the mushrooms with the rest of the ingredients in a large mixing bowl. Transfer the vegetables to a roasting tray and roast the vegetables for about 40 minutes until they are cooked through and a little crispy.

Serves 6

Cook's Note
This salad can be served hot or at room temperature. For added indulgence top with shaved parmesan and toasted pine nuts.

Mediterranean Potato Salad

- 2 kg Nicola potatoes
- 4 tbsp extra virgin olive oil
- 2 tbsp mayonnaise
- 100 g gherkins
- 1 red onion, finely diced
- 1 tsp salt
- 2 ml freshly ground black pepper
- 120 g black Calamata olives
- 20 g Italian flat-leaf parsley, chopped finely

Boil the potatoes in their skins until they are just cooked through. In the meantime mix together the olive oil, mayonnaise, gherkins, onions, salt and pepper. As soon as the potatoes are ready, cut them into chunks with the skin on and dress them with the olive oil mix. Pit the olives and tear them in half roughly and mix into the salad. Garnish with the freshly chopped parsley.

Serves 8 – 10

Cook's Note

It is important to use Mediterranean-style Nicola potatoes for their waxy texture and the way they hold their shape when sliced and also to dress the potatoes while they're still hot so that they absorb all the flavours in the dressing. This salad can be served hot or cold.

Cranberry and Goat's Cheese Salad

Growing up we never had fruit in salads but I absolutely love this combination, especially with the tartness of the goat's cheese.

- 150 g mixed baby lettuce leaves
- 100 g goat's cheese
- 60 g cranberries
- 40 g blueberries
- 40 g pine nuts, toasted

DRESSING
- 75 ml olive oil
- 60 ml good quality balsamic vinegar
- 1 tsp sugar
- 2 ml salt
- pinch of freshly ground black pepper

To make the dressing, combine all the ingredients together in a bowl. Place the baby leaves on a flattish platter, crumble the goat's cheese over them and sprinkle with the cranberries and blueberries. When you are ready to serve the salad, sprinkle the pine nuts over the top and pour the dressing all over.

Serves 6 – 8

Cook's Note
Add freshly sliced avocado to the salad when in season.

Artichoke and Red Kidney Bean Salad

A good basic salad to which you could add other vegetables, such as aubergines, green beans or peppers. Or just serve as part of a mezze.

- 500 g fresh artichoke quarters
- 500 ml olive oil
- 200 ml lemon juice
- 1 tsp sugar
- pinch of salt and freshly ground black pepper to taste
- 200 g red kidney beans
- 1 handful fresh origanum

Marinate the artichokes in the olive oil, lemon juice, sugar, salt and pepper overnight (they will keep for a month in the fridge).

Soak the beans overnight in 3 times the amount of water. Cook the beans the next day in water until tender. Strain and allow the beans to cool completely. Add the beans and the origanum leaves (broken up by hand) and mix through.

Serves 8 – 10

Cook's Note
Always use dried beans rather than tinned as they give a much better texture – almost silkiness – to this salad. Be sure not to add salt to the water when boiling the beans as it will make them chewy. If you like garlic, add a whole clove to the marinade. This salad will keep well for at least a week and is actually best eaten a few days after preparation.

Spicy Sweet Potato Salad with
Feta, Rocket and Toasted Seeds

- pinch of salt and freshly ground black pepper to taste
- 1 tsp paprika
- 1 tsp dried origanum
- 1 tsp cayenne pepper
- 2 cloves of garlic, crushed
- 3 tbsp extra virgin olive oil
- 700 g sweet potato, cut into wedges
- 40 g wild rocket
- 120 g Danish feta cheese
- 20 g sunflower seeds, toasted
- 20 g pumpkin seeds, toasted
- 50 g pomegranate seeds (when in season)
- Greek yoghurt or labneh and extra virgin olive oil for serving

Preheat the oven to 180°C.

Combine the salt, pepper, paprika, origanum, cayenne pepper, garlic and olive oil.

Cover the sweet potato wedges with this paste and roast in the oven until they are cooked through and golden brown. When you are ready to serve the salad, assemble it by mixing the rocket and sweet potato together on a platter. Top it off with crumbled feta cheese, the toasted seeds and the pomegranate seeds.

This salad is great served as is or accompanied by some Greek yoghurt or labneh and a generous drizzle of extra virgin olive oil.

Serves 4 – 6

Beetroot and Carrot Salad with Basil-Mint Yoghurt

I love raw fresh beetroot and can just munch on it as is – here it makes a light, summery salad.

- 600 g beetroot, peeled and grated
- 350 g carrots, peeled and grated
- 2 tbsp olive oil
- 2 tbsp red wine vinegar
- 50 ml honey
- pinch of salt and freshly ground pepper to taste
- 40 g rocket

DRESSING
- 150 g Greek yoghurt
- 20 g basil, finely sliced
- 10 g mint, chopped
- 1 tbsp lemon juice
- 40 ml olive oil
- pinch of salt and freshly ground black pepper to taste

Mix the beetroot, carrot, olive oil, red wine vinegar, honey, salt and pepper together.
For the dressing simply combine all the ingredients together. When you are ready to serve the salad, toss the rocket with the salad and put it on a platter. Top the salad with the yoghurt dressing and serve.

Serve 6 – 8

Cook's Note
For an added crunch, top the salad with some toasted seeds of your choice.

Cucumber and Green Bean Salad
with Cream Cheese and Poppyseeds

- 300 g fine green beans, halved
- 200 g baby corn, sliced
- 160 g hand-shelled fresh peas
- 1 cucumber, cut into chunks
- 1 red onion, sliced
- 100 ml cream cheese
- 10 g dill
- 10 g Italian flat-leaf parsley
- 80 ml poppy seeds
- 100 ml olive oil
- 1 lemon, juiced
- pinch of salt and freshly ground black pepper to taste

Mix the green beans, baby corn, fresh peas, cucumber and red onion together in a bowl. Prepare the dressing by blending the cream cheese with the dill and parsley.

Add the cream cheese mix to the vegetables with the poppy seeds, olive oil, lemon juice, salt and pepper. Mix all the ingredients together well and serve.

Serves 6 - 8

Fresh Green Salad with Lemon Dressing

Here blanched cauliflower, broccoli, cucumber and mangetout are almost pickled in a lemon dressing.

- 1 head broccoli, cut into florets
- 1 head cauliflower, cut into florets
- 100 g mangetout
- 1 English cucumber
- 100 ml lemon juice
- 80 ml olive oil
- pinch of salt and freshly ground black pepper to taste
- 50 g spring onions, thinly sliced

Blanche the broccoli, cauliflower and mangetout separately. Peel the cucumber and cut into long chunks.

To make the dressing combine the lemon juice with the olive oil, salt and pepper.

To assemble the salad, mix the blanched vegetables with the cucumber and dressing.

Plate the vegetables and decorate with the spring onion slices.

Serves 6 – 8

Quinoa and Vegetable Salad

We only started cooking with quinoa quite recently at Sababa and people love it – I think because it's so healthy. Quinoa is quite bland so it's all about what you add that makes it exciting – in this case, lots of grilled veggies.

- 1 kg quinoa
- 1 red pepper, cubed
- 1 yellow pepper, cubed
- 1 green pepper, cubed
- 1 red onion, quartered
- 2 large carrots, sliced at an angle
- 300 g baby marrows, sliced
- 1 head broccoli, cut into florets
- 4 tbsp extra virgin olive oil
- 1 tbsp salt
- 2 ml freshly ground black pepper
- zest and the juice of 1 lemon
- handful of dill, chopped
- handful of Italian flat-leaf parsley, chopped
- 60 g wild rocket
- 125 ml dried cranberries

Boil the quinoa in water for about 10 minutes. Roast the peppers, onions, carrots and baby marrows with the olive oil, salt and pepper until they are cooked through and golden brown. Blanche the broccoli in boiling water.

Once the quinoa has cooled down, mix through the lemon zest and juice, as well as the chopped herbs. Then add half the vegetables and toss, half the cranberries and all the rocket.

Plate the salad on a platter and garnish with the remaining vegetables and cranberries.

Serves 10 - 12

Green Bean and Baby Marrow Salad
with Rocket, Shaved Parmesan and Pine Nuts

- 350 g fine green beans, halved
- 350 g baby marrows, sliced thinly
- 1 lemon, juiced
- 2 tbsp extra virgin olive oil
- pinch of salt and freshly ground black pepper to taste
- 40 g wild rocket
- 20 g parmesan
- 20 g pine nuts, toasted

Blanche the greens by leaving them in boiling water for a few minutes and immediately after running them under cold water. Add 1 tablespoon of olive oil, a pinch of salt and freshly ground pepper to the baby marrow slices.

Roast the baby marrows in the oven at 180°C until they go slightly golden.

To assemble the salad simply dress the green beans and baby marrows with the lemon, olive oil, salt and pepper. Then mix the vegetables together with the rocket and plate onto a salad platter. Top it off with some parmesan shavings and toasted pine nuts.

Serves 4 – 6

Green Bean Salad with Char-Grilled Courgettes and Chickpeas

- 250 g dried chickpeas
- 400 g baby marrows, sliced thinly
- 300 g green beans, blanched
- 20 g Italian flat-leaf parsley
- 20 g fresh mint
- 100 ml extra virgin olive oil
- 20 ml red wine vinegar
- 20 ml lemon juice
- 30 g wild rocket
- 2 spring onions, thinly sliced
- pinch of salt and freshly ground black pepper to taste

Soak the chickpeas overnight in 3 times the amount of water. Strain them through a colander and rinse under cold water. Then boil the chickpeas in water for about half an hour until they are soft.

Chargrill the baby marrows in a griddle pan until they are just cooked through and the char marks are visible.

For the dressing mix together the olive oil, red wine vinegar, lemon juice, herbs, salt and pepper.

When you are ready to serve the salad, dress the chickpeas, green beans, and baby marrows with the dressing. Plate the vegetables with the rocket, and garnish with spring onions.

Serves 4 – 6

Shakshuka

This is a North African dish of eggs poached in spicy tomato sauce and the ingredients are basics you're always likely to have in the house: onions, garlic, tomatoes and eggs but you could embellish it by adding peppers, aubergines or potatoes.

- 1 onion, diced
- 2 tbsp vegetable oil
- 3 cloves of garlic, crushed
- 1 small red chilli, sliced (optional)
- 1 red pepper, diced
- 1 green pepper, diced
- 5 large overripe tomatoes, chopped
- 1 tsp sugar
- pinch of salt and freshly ground black pepper to taste
- 250 – 500 ml water
- 4 – 6 eggs
- 1 tsp cumin
- basic white bread for serving

Fry the onions in oil until they soften. Add the garlic and chilli and then the peppers, tomatoes, sugar, salt, pepper and 250 ml of water. Cook for about 20 minutes on a low heat until the sauce reduces slightly and the flavours have had time to develop.

If you find the sauce is too thick, add more water. Crack the eggs into the pan and continue cooking for about 10 minutes until they are cooked through. Sprinkle with cumin and serve with white bread.

Serves 3 – 4

Cook's Note

For a rich, flavourful sauce it's important to use ripe, red tomatoes when making it in summer and good quality tinned tomatoes when making it in winter.

HERZL'S SPECIALITIES

No matter what our dad does, he likes to do it properly. So, he will only cook when he's got the time, which is usually on a Sunday. He would make breakfast for us on a Sunday morning and shakshuka or minestra for Sunday night supper, dishes my mother would never make because they are his speciality. He also takes care of all the braai duties – if my mother is making pickled peppers or aubergines, it's always dad's job to char-grill the vegetables.

Sunday breakfasts started when I was about 12 and all four children were still living at home. My dad didn't like seeing us filling up on toast – he wanted to give us a healthy breakfast – so he would spend ages finely chopping pineapple for fruit salads with raspberries and figs, or removing all the pith from grapefruit to serve as juicy segments, or dicing tomato, cucumber and yellow pepper for Israeli salad.

We hardly ever had dessert – only fruit. After dinner he would sit peeling a bowl of oranges or slicing up sweet melon. And if we had guests for Friday night supper, it was dad's duty to cut all the fruit before everyone arrived so it was ready to serve – it's something he still does. I don't know about my siblings but I find it's a real effort to peel fruit because it's not something we ever did ourselves!

Dad was also in charge of all the fruit and vegetable buying. As a boy he worked on farms picking fruit to earn pocket money, so he has a good understanding of the seasons and what and how to buy. Because there were six of us, we went through a lot of produce and we had to store it wherever we had space – I remember once, as a child, having five enormous watermelons under my bed!

Our dad is very particular about where his food comes from and how it is made. He will still wake up early on a Sunday to gather everything for breakfast. And his breakfast rolls are a careful construction of each filling in just the right quantities and order: Israeli salad, thinly sliced and seasoned avocado, ricotta, pilpel-chuma (a chilli-garlic-paprika paste made by his mom) and in the middle, a fried egg straight from the pan.

PULSES & GRAINS

How to cook plain rice

We use Jasmine rice because we like its sticky sheen. We also fry off our rice before boiling and steam it after boiling. To cook rice the Sababa way, add 1½ tsp oil to the pot in which you're going to cook your rice and heat over a high heat. Add one cup of rice and cook, stirring, until the rice is toasted. Then add 1 tsp powdered vegetable or chicken stock (we use Telma) and a pinch of salt and pepper and stir through. Add 1½ cups of water and bring to the boil. Cook over a medium heat with the lid slightly ajar, stirring occasionally, until all the water is absorbed. We were taught by my mom, who learned from our grandparents (on both sides), that once all the water has been absorbed it's important to let the rice steam. Lift the lid, put a cloth over the pot, replace the lid and let it steam for a good 20 minutes. You can leave the cloth there until you're ready to serve it – the whole day if you like – but for a minimum of 15 to 20 minutes.

Magadreh

This is one of my favourite recipes and something we ate quite a lot of at home. It is best eaten warm and is usually served as a side – although the lentils make it so hearty I could eat bowls of magadreh just as it is. The trick is to cook your onions until soft, shiny and golden brown to get a good caramelised flavour.

- 500 ml small brown lentils
- 5 onions, sliced
- 125 ml vegetable oil
- 2 ml freshly ground black pepper
- 3 cups basmati rice
- 3 tbsp vegetable oil
- 2 tbsp vegetable stock powder
- 1 tsp salt and freshly ground black pepper to taste
- 4½ cups water

Cook's Note
The onions can cook gently for up to 45 minutes, just be careful that they don't burn by stirring every now and then.

Cook the lentils by boiling them in 3 times the amount of water until they are just soft.

In a frying pan, fry the onions with 125 ml oil, 1 teaspoon of salt and 2 ml of freshly ground black pepper until they are soft and dark brown in colour. The frying of the onions will take at least 15 minutes and you will need to stir them every so often to make sure they don't burn.

In order to prepare the rice heat 3 tbsp of vegetable oil in a pot. Add the rice and mix through. Add the vegetable stock and the remaining salt and pepper and continue to stir. Once the rice has been well-coated with the oil, add the lentils and 4½ cups of water. Bring the pot to the boil and then lower the heat and allow the rice to cook and absorb all the water. Make sure to give the rice a stir every so often so that the rice does not stick to the bottom of the pot and burn. Once the rice is cooked, turn the heat off, cover the pot with a clean cloth and then place the lid on top. Leave the rice to steam for at least 20 minutes before opening the pot. Check the seasoning of the rice and when you are ready to serve, cover the rice all over with the fried onions.

Serves 10 – 12

Couscous and Tirshi

Couscous forms the basis of Libyan cuisine because it is so good at absorbing the sauce from all those stews that the Libyans love to cook. Couscous is an accompaniment to almost everything we eat, and most of the time, when we have couscous, our mother will also make tirshi: a zesty mash of butternut, carrots and baby marrow, seasoned with cumin, paprika, garlic and extra virgin olive oil. The couscous-tirshi combination is particularly delicious with meat dishes – I would definitely recommend it with our lamb knuckle stew and it is typically served with mafrum.

COUSCOUS
- 4 cups water
- 80 ml sunflower oil
- 1 tbsp chicken or vegetable stock
- pinch of salt and freshly ground black pepper to taste
- 4 cups couscous
- 100 g butter

TIRSHI
- 300 g baby marrows
- 200 g carrots
- 600 g butternut
- 2 cups water
- 125 ml canola oil
- 7 cloves of garlic, crushed
- 2 tsp paprika
- 2 tsp cumin
- 1 lemon
- pinch of salt and freshly ground black pepper to taste

For the couscous, bring the water to the boil with the oil, stock, salt and pepper. Add the couscous all at once and mix through. Turn the heat off and leave the couscous in the pot for a short while with the lid on. Add the butter and, using a fork, break the couscous up so that it doesn't become lumpy. Then put the lid back on and leave the couscous to steam in the pot.

For the tirshi, prepare the baby marrows, carrots and butternut by peeling them and cutting them into chunks. Put the vegetables in a pot with the water and simmer for about half an hour until all the vegetables are soft. Make sure that the carrots are soft as they take the longest to cook through properly.

In the meantime mix together the oil with the garlic, paprika, cumin, lemon and salt and pepper.

Once the vegetables are cooked through, mash them up together with the rest of the ingredients.

Serves 8 – 10

Cook's Note
The couscous is best served warm and the tirshi at room temperature.

Chickpea Stew

- 500 g dried chickpeas
- 2 onions, diced
- 2 tbsp vegetable oil
- 1 tbsp garlic, crushed
- 1 tbsp turmeric
- 2 tsp paprika
- pinch of salt and freshly ground black pepper to taste
- 1 tbsp vegetable stock powder mixed with 1 litre water
- 2 handfuls of coriander, chopped

Soak the chickpeas overnight in 3 times the amount of water. The next day drain the chickpeas through a colander and rinse with cold water.

Using a pot, fry the onions with the oil until they are soft and translucent. Then add the garlic and mix for a minute. Add the turmeric, paprika, salt and pepper and mix again. Add the chickpeas and then the stock. Bring the pot to the boil and then simmer for about an hour until the chickpeas are soft and the liquid has reduced slightly. Lastly mix through the coriander.

Serves 6 - 8

SAVOURY PIES,
PASTRIES & BAKES

Roast Tomato, Olive and Goat's Cheese Tart

This tart makes a great starter for dinner parties because it can be prepared in advance and then baked when your guests arrive.

- 400 g puff pastry
- 20 cherry tomatoes
- 1 tbsp extra virgin olive oil
- 1 onion
- 2 tbsp vegetable oil
- 10 Calamata olives, pitted
- 100 g goat's cheese
- 1 sprig fresh origanum, chopped
- 1 egg, beaten
- pinch of salt and freshly ground black pepper to taste
- extra virgin olive oil
- wild rocket for serving

Line a 24-cm tart tin with puff pastry and leave it to rest in the fridge until you are ready to bake it.

Preheat the oven to 180°C and roast the tomatoes with the olive oil and a pinch of salt and pepper until the tomatoes are soft and slightly brown.

In the meantime, slice the onion and fry it with the vegetable oil and a pinch of salt and pepper until the onions are golden brown and soft.

Once this is ready, take the prepared tart tin out the fridge, top it with the tomatoes, pitted Calamata olives, fried onions and slices of goat's cheese. Sprinkle some origanum leaves and freshly ground black pepper over the vegetables. Lastly brush the pastry lightly with some beaten egg. Bake the tart in the oven for about 30 minutes until the pastry is golden and cooked through. Serve the tart warm with a drizzle of extra virgin olive oil and some fresh wild rocket.

Serves 6

Spinach, Mushroom and Onion Bake

Our mom never baked much for us growing up but her mushroom pie, or pashtida as it's called in Hebrew, sticks in my memory. This bake is not her own recipe but was inspired but her mushroom pie.

- 1 kg Swiss chard
- 3 onions, sliced
- 100 – 150 ml sunflower oil
- 700 g button mushrooms, sliced
- 2 eggs
- 2 egg yolks
- 1 cup cream
- salt and freshly ground black pepper

Cook's Note

For a dairy-free version omit the cream and substitute one extra egg plus one yolk. You could also finish the bake by topping with grated mozzarella, cheddar or feta before it goes into the oven.

Preheat the oven to 180°C.

Cook the spinach in batches in a large pan with a teaspoon of oil and a pinch of salt and pepper each time. Once all the spinach is cooked, leave it to cool in a colander to allow all the liquid from the spinach to strain off. Then chop the spinach finely.

In the meantime, fry the onions with 50 ml of vegetable oil and a pinch of salt and pepper until they are soft and brown. In another pan, cook the mushrooms with 50 ml of oil and a pinch of salt and pepper until all the liquid from the mushrooms has been released and they are golden brown.

Put all the vegetables together in a mixing bowl and mix with the eggs, egg yolks and cream. Check the seasoning and adjust it with more salt and pepper if necessary.

Transfer the mixture to a baking dish and bake for about 30 – 40 minutes until the bake has set and has a nice golden brown colour.

Serves 8 – 10

Butternut and Blue Cheese Quiche

Whenever someone tells me they don't like quiche, I always say just try our quiche. Ours isn't a rich, egg quiche – it is more of a vegetable tart with just enough egg to hold everything together. The quiches fly out the shop over the summer season because they keep well, are easy to serve and can be eaten either hot or at room temperature.

- 400 g puff pastry
- 700 g butternut
- 2 tbsp olive oil
- 100 g blue cheese
- 50 g mozzarella cheese
- 35 g cheddar cheese
- 3 egg yolks
- 1 egg
- 1 cup cream
- pinch of salt and freshly ground black pepper to taste
- 30 g pumpkin seeds

Cook's Note

If you find the quiche is getting too brown on top and the pastry is not cooking through, then once it's cooled down a little, flip it over onto an oven proof tray, remove the tart tin and bake further upside down. Once the pastry is sufficiently cooked, remove from the oven and turn right side up.

Line a 20-cm quiche tin with puff pastry and leave it in the fridge to cool.

Preheat the oven to 180°C.

Cut the butternut into small cubes and mix together with the olive oil and a pinch of salt and pepper. Roast the butternut in the oven until soft and golden.

In the meantime, grate the cheddar and mozzarella and prepare the quiche filling by whisking the egg with the yolks, cream and a pinch of salt and pepper. Once the butternut has cooled down slightly, place evenly over the pastry. Add the blue cheese, mozzarella and cheddar and then pour in the quiche filling. Sprinkle with the pumpkin seeds and bake the quiche for about 30 minutes until the pastry has a nice golden brown colour and the pastry has cooked through.

Serves 6 – 8

'People are obsessed with bourekitas, it's impossible to stop eating them and Sababa Sea Point sells mountains of these little pies!' – Nirit

BOUREKITAS

Bourekas are savoury pies made with puff, phyllo or shortcrust pastry and filled with mushrooms, cheese, potato, spinach or aubergine. They originally came from Turkey and Greece but you find them all over Israel in various sizes with the kind of seed sprinkled over the top indicating what filling is inside.

At Sababa we make mini bourekas, which are called bourekitas and the best way to enjoy them is with a beer or an aperitif. It doesn't matter who comes over, it's one of those things everybody loves so you can never have enough stored in your freezer!

My mother-in-law, Jackie, is an expert bourekita-maker and she taught me how to make them the South African Sephardi way. Although Jackie is also Sephardi, her mother came from Turkey and her father from Rhodes Island in Greece, so her cooking is slightly different to the Sephardi food we know.

Whenever Jackie hears of someone who is sick or in need of comforting, she'll arrive at their door with a tray full of bourekitas. They're handrolled so you can't help but feel good when eating them because there's a lot of love that goes into the labour-intensive process of making them.

Potato and Cheese Bourekitas

- 1 cup water
- 1 cup sunflower oil
- 2 ml salt
- 4 – 5 cups flour

FILLING
- 500 g potatoes, boiled and peeled
- 1 cup mature cheddar, grated
- 30 g parmesan, grated
- 1 egg, beaten
- pinch of salt
- 1 egg for brushing
- sesame seeds for sprinkling

Prepare the dough by mixing together the water, oil and salt. Add enough flour all at once to make a firm dough. Knead the dough a little and then shape it into walnut sized balls. Allow the dough to rest for 10 minutes.

Prepare the filling by mashing the potatoes and mixing them with the rest of the ingredients while they are still hot.

Roll out each ball to about 6 cm in diameter and place a tablespoonful of the filling in the centre of the pastry. Fold the pastry over to seal the filling, making sure the sides are tucked in as well.

Once you have prepared all the pastry and filling this way, line a baking tray with baking paper and brush each pastry with beaten egg. Sprinkle with sesame seeds and bake for 20 – 30 minutes on 170°C until golden brown.

Makes 30 – 40

The best boureka ever

The street food is good in Israel and when we travel there with our parents they always take us to these hole-in-the-wall places that serve the best versions of their favourite things. When Russell came over to meet my extended family, my father wanted to show him (and us, of course) the best boureka in Israel. So he took us all the way to Haifa, to a tiny shack on the side of a busy highway. There were openings on either side. One faced the pavement, where you could stand and eat, and the other was a hatch with a clear PVC flap facing the road and creating a boreka drive-through – a car or truck would slow down and the driver would grab a packet of borekas from the hatch before driving off again. The guy makes the same amount of borekas every morning and his day ends when he sells out, which is usually around 9 am. We could smell the borekas, which are served warm and sliced, with a hard-boiled egg, olives, Israeli salad and zhoug (chilli sauce). We could taste how fresh they were, they were baked to perfection. Good, handmade pastry is often what defines a good boreka, and this pastry was like no other. It was, seriously, the best boureka any of us had ever tasted.

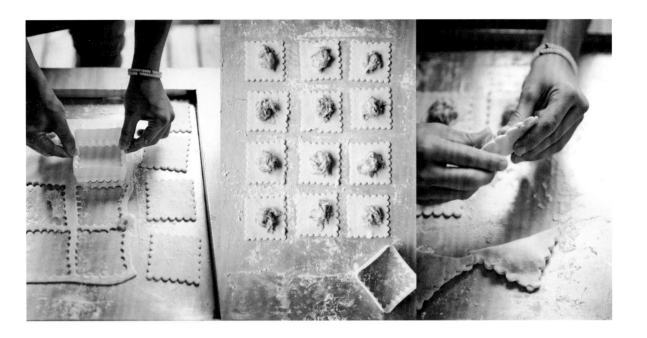

Leek and Cheese Pies

- 300 g leeks, chopped
- 2 tbsp sunflower oil
- 1 tsp garlic, crushed
- 10 ml thyme
- pinch of salt and freshly ground black pepper to taste
- 1 tsp salted butter
- 50 g goat's cheese
- 100 g cream cheese
- 2 sheets puff pastry
- flour
- 1 egg for brushing
- sesame seeds for sprinkling

For the filling, fry the leeks in the oil until they go soft and translucent. Add the garlic, thyme, salt and pepper and continue cooking for about 10 minutes until all the flavours have come together. Then add the butter and mix through.

Allow this mixture to cool down and then add the goat's cheese and cream cheese.

Flour a working surface and lay out the sheets of puff pastry.

Using an 8-cm square pastry cutter, cut out as many square as you can from 1 sheet.

Brush water all around the edges of the squares and place a tablespoon full of the leek and cheese filling in the middle of each square. Close the squares by sealing the edges to form triangles and then place the pies onto a baking tray lined with baking paper.

Brush the pies with beaten egg and sprinkle with sesame seeds.

Bake the pies at 170°C for about 30 minutes until the pastry is golden brown and cooked through.

Makes 30

Mushroom Pie Logs

This Sababa innovation uses mushrooms and lots of onions wrapped up to make one big puff pie – our mom always cooks with a lot of onions to lend sweetness.

- 6 tbsp sunflower oil
- 3 onions, sliced
- 600 g mushrooms, sliced
- pinch of salt and freshly ground black pepper to taste
- 400 g puff pastry
- 1 egg, beaten
- sesame seeds

Heat the oil in a frying pan and fry the onions with the salt and pepper until they are golden brown. Add the mushrooms and continue cooking until all the liquid from the mushrooms has evaporated and the mushrooms are golden brown. Allow to cool.

Roll out the puff pastry with a rolling pin and stretch the pastry into an oblong shape. Place the mushroom mixture along the length of the pastry along the edge closest to you. Starting with the side that has the filling along it, roll the pastry over to form a log-shaped pie, tucking the sides in as you roll.

Line a baking tray with baking paper and then place the pie onto it. Leave the pie to cool in the fridge for at least an hour before baking.

Preheat the oven to 170°C.

Remove the pie from the fridge and with a sharp knife score the pie at intervals along the width, cutting almost all the way through each time. Brush the pie with egg and sprinkle sesame seeds over the top. Bake the pie in the oven until the pastry is golden brown and cooked all the way through.

Serves 6 – 8

Aubergine Bake with Tomato, Parmesan and Basil

This is similar to aubergine parmigiana but with a Libyan-Italian influence from our dad's side of the family.

- 5 – 6 medium aubergines, cut into wedges
- extra virgin olive oil for brushing
- pinch of salt and freshly ground black pepper to taste
- 80 g parmesan, grated
- 200 g mozzarella, grated
- 1 handful basil leaves

SAUCE
- 2 tbsp vegetable oil
- 2 onions, diced
- 2 cloves garlic, crushed
- pinch of salt and freshly ground black pepper to taste
- 1 tsp paprika
- pinch cinnamon
- 2 ml cumin
- 70 g tomato paste
- 820 g tinned chopped tomatoes
- 1 cup water
- 2 tsp sugar

Preheat the oven to 180°C.

Cut the aubergines into medium-thickness wedges. Sprinkle salt over the aubergine wedges and after 10 minutes, wash and dry them. Put the wedges flat down onto the baking tray. Brush each wedge with olive oil and sprinkle with salt and freshly ground black pepper. Roast the aubergines in the oven until they are soft, browned and slightly crisp.

In the meantime prepare the sauce. Fry the onions in the oil until they go soft and translucent. Add the garlic and then all the spices. Mix through for about a minute and then add the tomato paste, tinned tomatoes, water and sugar. Bring the sauce to the boil and then gently simmer for about 30 minutes, stirring occasionally.

Once the aubergine wedges and sauce are ready, layer the aubergines with the sauce in a casserole dish, making sure that there is enough sauce for the top layer. Then cover the top layer with grated mozzarella and parmesan, and decorate with the basil leaves.

About 45 minutes before you are ready to eat, preheat the oven to 180°C and bake for about 20 – 30 minutes, until the cheese has melted and the top is golden brown.

Serves 6 – 8

Chicken Pasta Bake

At Sababa we prepare a number of different lasagnes for people to take home and bake at home. This is one of the favourites.

- 500 g penne
- 2 onions, diced
- 4 tbsp vegetable oil
- 1 tsp turmeric
- 1 tsp cumin
- 500 g chicken breast, cubed
- 1 tsp chicken spice
- 1 tsp chicken stock powder
- 1 green pepper, diced
- 1 red pepper, diced
- 1 yellow pepper, diced
- 2 green chillies, chopped (if you like it hot, then keep the seeds)
- 300 g mushrooms, sliced
- pinch of salt and freshly ground black pepper to taste
- 300 g mozzarella, grated
- 2 sprigs fresh origanum

BÉCHAMEL SAUCE
- 100 g butter
- 100 g flour
- 1 litre milk
- pinch of salt and freshly ground black pepper to taste

Start by cooking the pasta until *al dente*. Fry the onions in a pan with 2 tbsp of oil until they soften. Then add the turmeric, cumin and chicken, and continue cooking until the chicken has cooked through. Add the chicken spice and chicken stock and mix through. Set the chicken aside and in the same pan cook the peppers, chillies and mushrooms in the remaining oil until soft.

Then prepare the béchamel sauce. Melt the butter in a pot and then add the flour all at once. Cook the butter and flour together for a few minutes and then add the milk, salt and pepper. Turn the heat down slightly and whisk the mixture continuously until the sauce thickens and you can no longer taste the flour.

At this stage you can combine the pasta with the béchamel sauce, chicken and vegetables, and adjust the seasoning if necessary. Transfer the mixture to an ovenproof dish, sprinkle with the grated mozzarella and then add the fresh origanum leaves.

Bake the pasta bake in the oven for about 20 – 30 minutes at 180°C until the mozzarella has melted and is a golden brown colour.

Serves 8 - 10

Sweet Potato and Butternut Bake

- 800 g sweet potato, thinly sliced
- 1 onion, sliced
- 1 kg butternut, peeled and thinly sliced
- 1 cup cream
- 1 tbsp thyme, chopped
- pinch of salt and freshly ground black pepper to taste
- 60 g Danish feta cheese

Preheat the oven to 180°C.

Put the sweet potato, onion and butternut slices in a large mixing bowl. Blend together the cream with the thyme, salt and pepper in a separate bowl.

Place the vegetables in a casserole dish, making sure they are packed tightly together.

Pour the cream mixture over the vegetables, making sure all the vegetable slices are well coated, then sprinkle with the feta cheese.

Cover the dish with foil and bake for about 45 minutes or until the vegetables are cooked through. Remove the foil and bake for another 20 - 30 minutes until the top is golden brown.

Serves 8

Farfalle with Baby Spinach, Char-Grilled Vegetables, Ricotta and Pine Nuts

- 1 large aubergine
- 2 large baby marrows
- 500 g farfalle
- extra virgin olive oil
- 1 tsp garlic, crushed
- pinch of salt and freshly ground black pepper to taste
- 250 g Calamata olives, pitted
- 1 red onion, sliced
- 200 g baby spinach leaves
- 300 g ricotta cheese
- 30 g pine nuts, toasted in a dry pan
- 125 ml parmesan, freshly grated

Prepare the aubergines and baby marrows by cutting them in thin slices. Brush them with olive oil and then char-grill them on a griddle pan with a little salt and pepper.

Boil the pasta until *al dente* and then while still hot, toss with half a cup extra virgin olive oil, garlic, salt, pepper, pitted olives, red onion and the baby spinach. Add the char-grilled vegetables, ricotta and pine nuts and toss through.

Dress the pasta with a little more extra virgin olive oil and sprinkle with the grated parmesan shavings.

Serves 8 – 10

Za'atar

Za'atar is a hardy herb that grows in the Middle-Eastern countries. You can cook with it whole but it's often sold crushed and – like the spices – the fresher it's crushed, the better it is. Za'atar is quite bitter so it's often available as part of a spice mix, often in combination with salt, sumac and sesame. It can be sprinkled over salads or used to season chicken breasts, and when I was learning how to make pita breads, my uncle took me to a pita factory in an Arab village where they used fresh za'atar leaves, toasted in olive oil, in their pitas. We import the za'atar that we use from Israel.

Pesach Frittata

Over Pesach (Jewish Passover) regular bread cannot be eaten and is replaced with matzo (unleavened bread) for the seven days of the festival. This is an important festival which remembers the Jewish exodus from Egypt and the following 40 years of life in the desert. After a while plain matzo with egg becomes boring. Our mother's recipe is a more spicy and interesting version. She adds cumin and za'atar and turns it into a frittata, adding sweet potato to give some substance. It's lovely all year round, cut into wedges and served with a green, leafy, salad. (*See also* Matzo cake in the next section.)

- 4 slices of matzo
- 1 tbsp vegetable oil
- half an onion, sliced
- 100 g butternut, peeled and cut into strips
- 100 g sweet potato, peeled and cut into strips
- 1 tsp thyme, chopped
- 4 eggs
- 20 g Danish feta
- 1 tsp za'atar
- pinch of salt and freshly ground black pepper to taste
- extra virgin olive oil for drizzling

Wet the matzo slices under running tap water and leave them to soften for a few minutes. Heat the oil in a frying pan and cook the onions, butternut and sweet potato with the thyme until they go slightly golden and crispy.

In the meantime, whisk the eggs together and crumble the matzo into the mixture with the salt and pepper. Add the egg mixture to the pan and cook the frittata for a few minutes on each side. Transfer the frittata onto a plate, sprinkle with the za'atar and crumble the feta over. Drizzle with some extra virgin olive oil and serve with a salad.

Serves 4

SWEETS & CAKES

Garinim
There were always seeds and nuts in our home and all over Israel you'll find market vendors selling nuts, seeds, olives and dried fruit. Even when you walk into the local neighbourhood cafés, the first things you will see are glassed-in, heated sections dedicated to toasted seeds and nuts. A common snack is garinim, which consists of sunflower seeds, watermelon seeds and pumpkin seeds all in the shells, toasted and salted. When visiting Israel my parents bring back kilos at a time and every night after dinner our dad will have two small bowls in front of him, one full of seeds and one for the shells.

More than cakes, in Israeli culture the focus is on fruit and nuts. There are excellent quality dried figs and dates available, and the Moroccans, for instance, use them to make sweets like almond-stuffed dates. So we might have those for dessert, as opposed to a pudding, as well as plenty of fresh-cut, seasonal fruit.

For this reason we use a lot of fruit, nuts and seeds in our baking, making frangipane-filled tarts, poppy seed and almond-based cakes, and sprinkling our white chocolate and coconut rugelach with white sesame seeds. We do make other things for the shop because people ask for them, like chocolate brownies and baked cheesecake, but whatever we do, we only do it because it is a good version of that cake.

'In Israel, dates are like the aubergine of the sweet world!' – Nirit

Poppy Seed Cake

- 4 eggs
- 1 ½ cups castor sugar
- 175 ml sunflower oil
- zest of 1 lemon
- 1 cup desiccated coconut
- 175 ml poppy seeds
- 1 cup self-raising flour
- 1 cup yoghurt

CAKE TOPPING
- 240 g white chocolate
- 50 ml cream
- raspberries for decoration (optional)
- icing sugar for dusting

Preheat the oven to 170°C.

Grease a 20-cm springform tin and line the base and sides with baking paper.

Beat the eggs and sugar together in a mixer until the mixture turns light and fluffy.

Add the oil in slowly on a low speed setting and then the lemon zest.

In a bowl mix all the dry ingredients together. Add this to the liquids and mix until well incorporated. Pour the mixture into the tin and bake for about 50 minutes until the cake is golden brown and baked through.

GANACHE TOPPING
To make the ganache, melt the chocolate over a double boiler. Then mix through the cream. Once the cake is cool, you can either dust it with icing sugar and serve as is, or spread the white chocolate ganache over the top and decorate with raspberries and icing sugar.

Serves 8 – 10

Frangipane and Nectarine Tart

- 1 egg
- 60 g icing sugar
- 250 g flour
- 1 ml salt
- 180 g unsalted butter, cold and cut into 5 mm squares

FRANGIPANE FILLING
- 250 g ground almonds
- 250 g icing sugar
- 250 g soft butter
- 4 eggs
- 125 g flour, sifted
- apricot jam
- nectarines, thinly sliced
- 3 tbsp icing sugar for dusting (optional)

For the pastry, beat the egg and icing sugar together. Put the flour and salt into a food processor and combine for a moment. Distribute the butter over the flour and pulse until just combined. Add the egg and icing sugar mix to the food processor and pulse again until the dough comes together.

Transfer the dough to a lightly floured surface and knead it until smooth, taking care not to overwork it. Wrap the dough in clingfilm and allow it to rest for an hour in the fridge.

In the meantime prepare the filling. Mix the almonds and icing sugar together. Beat the butter in a mixer until creamy. Add a third of the almond mix and beat well.

Add 1 egg and mix until pale in colour. Add another third of the almond mix and then add another egg and mix again. Add the last third of the almond mixture and then add the last of the eggs and mix well. Fold in the flour.

Have your tart tin of 28 – 30 cm with the removable bottom ready. Now roll out the pastry on a lightly floured surface to about 3 mm in thickness. To prevent the pastry from sticking to the counter and to ensure uniform thickness, keep lifting up and turning the pastry a quarter turn as you roll and always rolling from the centre of the pastry outwards. When the pastry is the desired size, lightly roll it around your rolling pin and then unroll it onto the tart tin. Lightly press the pastry into the bottom and up the sides of the tart tin, cutting off any excess pastry from the top of the tin. Spread a thin layer of the frangipane mixture on the pastry, then a thin layer of jam and then spread the rest of the frangipane mixture on top.

Decorate the tart with the nectarine slices. Starting from the outside edge and working inwards, place the nectarine slices almost one on top of the other so that they are slightly overlapping.

Bake the tart at 170°C for about 30 – 45 minutes until golden brown and baked through. Remove the tart from the oven and once it has cooled down slightly, take it out of the tin. Dust the tart with icing sugar and serve.

'Our grandmother, Golda, always had plenty of time – nothing was ever rushed – and that's why everything of hers always tasted so good. That and the air conditioning... in summer the house was always freezing so her pastry always kept crisp!' – Nirit

Apple and Almond Tart

- 400 g puff pastry
- 4 large granny smith apples
- 2 eggs
- 20 ml cornflour
- 100 g butter, melted
- 150 g flaked almonds
- 100 g castor sugar

Preheat oven to 170°C.

Line a 24-cm round tart tin with puff pastry and leave in the fridge to cool.

Peel and cut the apples into medium-size blocks. Whisk the eggs in a mixing bowl together with the cornflour, butter and sugar. Fill the lined tart tin with the apples, pour the sauce over the apples and then sprinkle the almonds over the top. Bake the tart in the oven for about 30 minutes until golden brown on top and the pastry has cooked through.

If you find the tart is getting too brown on top and the pastry has not cooked through, then once it has cooled down a little, flip it over onto an oven proof tray, remove the tart tin and continue to bake upside down in the oven. Once the pastry has cooked through, remove it from the oven and flip it right side up again.

Serves 6 – 8

Matzo Cake

There are some terrible cakes that come out over Passover – either with ingredients missing or made with matzo meal – because flour and raising agents aren't allowed. This one is made with whole matzo crackers and it is surprisingly good! Our mother makes it every Pesach (Passover) and keeps it in the fridge for the duration of the festival, so every time you need something sweet you can help yourself to a slice. The delicious flavour comes from the Kiddush wine – a sweet red wine drunk every Shabbat (Jewish Sabbath) or religious festival. The matzo is soaked in the wine, smeared with a salty, chocolate spread and stacked in layers before being left to set. The white, horizontal stripes of matzo look beautiful when sliced.

- 600 g matzo slices
- Kiddush (sweet) wine or rum for dipping
- 180 g dark chocolate
- 100 g butter
- 2 tbsp castor sugar
- 2 tbsp water
- 6 egg yolks
- pomegranate seeds for decorating

Dip the matzo slices in the wine or rum. Melt the chocolate, butter, sugar and water together in a saucepan and mix. Remove the saucepan from the heat and then whisk the egg yolks one at a time and add to the chocolate mixture. Spread the chocolate mixture onto each matzo slice and then place one on top of the next to form a stack. Make sure you keep enough chocolate spread to cover the top piece.

Decorate with the pomegranate seeds and leave to cool in the fridge for at least an hour before cutting.

Serve 8 – 10

Cook's Note
Rum or brandy can be substituted for the Kiddush wine. We've decorated the cake with pomegranate seeds here but crushed pistachios would also be nice.

Meringues

South Africans *love* meringues and buy ours to have with passion fruit or lemon curd and cream.

- 6 egg whites
- 2 ml lemon juice
- 1 tsp vanilla essence
- 360 g castor sugar

Cook's Note
If you prefer your meringues dry on the inside, leave them in the oven longer. We usually bake the meringues, turn the oven off and leave the meringues in the oven overnight. The meringues will keep for a few weeks if stored in an airtight container and kept in a dry place.

Preheat the oven to 110°C.

Place the egg whites in a mixing bowl and use the whisk attachment. Start to whisk on a low speed and once the whites have become a little foamy, add the lemon juice and vanilla. Continue whisking on medium speed, adding the sugar a teaspoon at a time until all the sugar has been well incorporated. The mixture should be thick and glossy and standing up in peaks. Spoon the mixture onto a baking sheet and bake in the oven for about 2 hours until crisp on the outside and chewy on the inside.

Makes about 15

Jackie and the Smith family

Although Russell and I were part of the same community and congregation in Cape Town, we didn't meet until we were introduced. Russell's mother, Jackie is Sephardi and his father Les is Ashkenazi, but he grew up eating his mother's family's food. He was brought up in the traditional Sephardi way and there has always been a love of good food in the Smith home. Russ so appreciates my mother's cooking and I feel the same way about his mom's food. Jackie is a talented cook and baker and she has taught me a lot since I became a part of the Smith family. Jackie is always cooking and baking for people; whether it's to say thank you, or to show kindness to someone in mourning, or during a time of celebration. Jackie and her family also show love, care and respect through their food.

Jackie's Florentines

My mother-in-law, Jackie Smith, showed us how to make these florentines. They are so easy and are a firm favourite – they are always one of the first items to be sold out on Sababa's sweet table.

- 4 cups corn flakes
- 2 cups unsalted peanuts
- 1 cup raisins
- 1 tin condensed milk
- 300 g good quality milk/ dark chocolate

Preheat the oven to 170°C.

Line a baking tray with baking paper. Mix all the ingredients together and place spoonfuls of the mixture slightly apart on the baking tray. Bake for about 8 minutes until golden brown. Allow the florentines to cool completely before peeling them off the baking sheet. Turn them upside down on the baking sheet.

Melt the chocolate and spread each one generously with the chocolate. Leave the chocolate to set by placing the florentines in the fridge or freezer for about an hour.

Makes 25 - 30

RUGELACH

Rugelach are pastries that look like baby croissants, with crème patissierre, finely chopped spiced nuts or dark chocolate folded through buttery yeast dough before it is rolled. They are an essential in Israel and at the markets you find them heaped in great big pyramids – the quantity is mind-boggling, but by the end of the day they're always all gone.

Every single town has a couple of bakeries selling rugelach but often these are pre-made, frozen, and supplied from a central factory. So there's something very special about having a rugela that's freshly made, by hand, like the ones Nirit makes.

Nirit learned how to make rugelach during her year working at Dallal bakery, where she spent six months rolling up to 200 a day. Dallal's rugelach are of a very high quality, they're lighter, more delicate and petite compared with the rustic and robust variety generally found in Israel.

As soon as Nirit moved back home, she began practising her rugelach and refining her recipe. It took quite a while to get it right because flour, water and weather all play a big role in producing the perfect pastry and all of those variables were different here, but I definitely think Nirit has perfected it.

Israelis may not be big on desserts but they will always have a little something sweet with their tea, or start their day with a coffee and a rugela. We had to introduce this morning concept to Capetonians and slowly but surely they were addicted!

Making rugelach is quite a complex process so it helps to have a good understanding of baking and yeast dough. Set aside at least two days as the dough needs to rest for 24 hours in the fridge and then there's the folding, which can be tricky at first and requires some practice to get right.

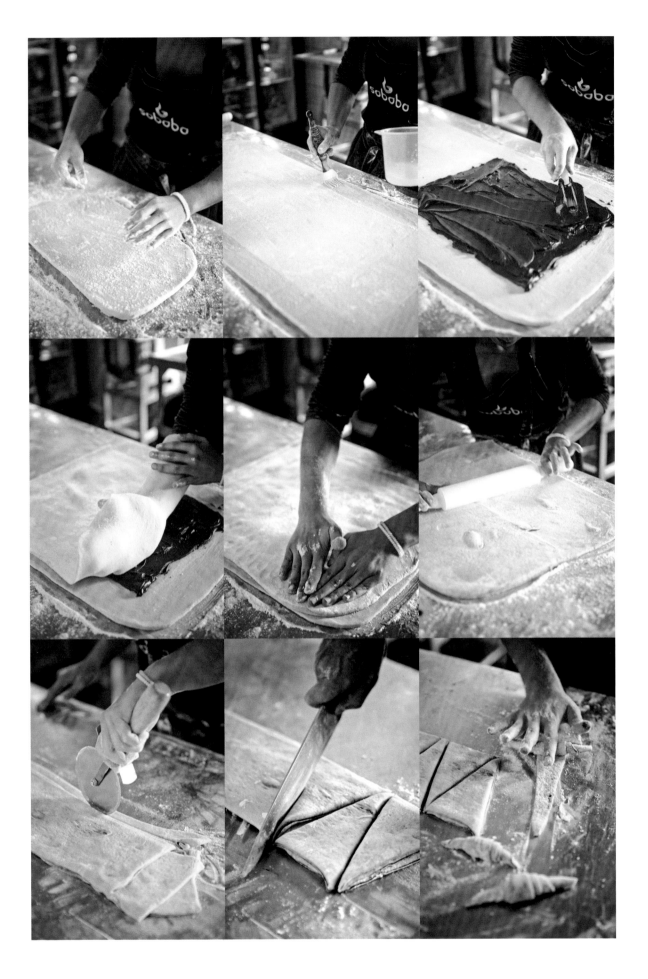

Rugelach

- 1 – 2 eggs, for brushing
- 1.25 kg white bread flour
- 20 g salt
- 20 g castor sugar
- 17 g dry yeast
- 118 g eggs (important to get the correct weight)
- 118 g sunflower oil
- 475 g mineral water
- 500 g butter, diced

SYRUP
- 250 g sugar
- 250 g water

FILLING
- 360 g dark chocolate
- 150 ml full cream milk
- 100 g cocoa powder, sifted

Start with the dough by placing all the liquids into the mixer. Then add the dry ingredients into the liquids and mix for 3 – 5 minutes on a medium speed until all the ingredients have come together. With the mixer on, add the butter one block at a time until the dough becomes soft and glossy.

Take the dough out of the mixer, knead it for a minute and then place it in a container, covered with cling wrap, in the fridge overnight.

Prepare the stock syrup by bringing the water and sugar to the boil. Once all the sugar has dissolved, turn the heat off and leave the syrup to cool.

The next day, prepare the filling by melting the chocolate and milk over a double boiler. Then add the sifted cocoa powder and mix together well. Leave the chocolate mixture to cool until it reaches room temperature.

Flour your work surface. Then divide the dough in half on the floured surface. Place half the dough back in the fridge until you are ready to use it again. Using the half that you are going to roll out, mould the dough into an even-sized square. With a rolling pin, stretch the dough out into an even rectangle. Brush half of the rectangle with water, which will help the dough to seal when you fold it over. Add half of the chocolate spread to the centre of the half of the dough that has the water brushed onto it.

Spread the chocolate evenly so that it fills that half. Then fold the dry half of the dough onto the chocolate half and pat the dough down to get all the air bubbles out and to seal the edges of the dough. Re-flour your work surface and roll the remaining dough again into its original size. Be gentle with the dough so that it doesn't tear. Cut the borders of the rectangle off and discard. Then cut the dough into 3 even-sized strips lengthways. Flour each strip and place the strips one on top of each other. Cut the strips into even-sized triangles for rolling. Roll each triangle from bottom to top so that it resembles the shape of a croissant.

Place the rugelach on a baking tray lined with baking paper and allow them to prove until they double in size.

Preheat the oven to 160°C. Brush the rugelach with the beaten egg and bake them for about 6 – 8 minutes. When they come out the oven, brush them twice with the stock syrup.

Makes 60 – 80

Cook's Note

You can skip the layering step and instead just spread each individual rectangle of dough with filling, cut each one into even-sized triangles and just roll up each triangle. This can get messy and the filling will be more exposed (you won't get those fine layers between the pastry) but you will have the same flavour and it's a far simpler way of doing it. This recipe makes a large quantity so you could freeze the rolled rugelach just before the final proving stage.

Garin is a seed in Hebrew and *garinem* is 'seeds' plural. You have to see how people eat them, especially while watching a soccer game – peels land up all over the place! My dad is very well practised in the art of eating seeds; he cracks the shells with his teeth so the seeds pop out, then there's a quick hand movement and he discards the shell. We all try to emulate his brilliant technique but have never had any success. I remember our parents saying when they came to South Africa their friends thought we were eating bird food because they'd only ever seen parrots eating sunflower seeds in the shell!' – Nirit

Chocolate Hazelnut Truffles

We don't do a wide range of baked goods but with whatever we do, we maintain a certain standard. Our cheesecake is rich and dense because we only use American-style cream cheese and for our truffles we only use Belgian Callebaut chocolate.

- 400 g good quality dark chocolate (with at least 70% cocoa solids)
- 400 ml cream
- 250 g hazelnuts, skinned

Cook's Note
Remember, your truffles will only taste as good as the chocolate you use. The truffles can be stored in the fridge but they are best eaten at room temperature.

Chop the chocolate finely. Heat the cream in a pot until it's about to boil.

Pour the cream over the chocolate and mix well until the mixture is smooth and there are no lumps. Leave the mixture to cool in the fridge for a few hours until it hardens enough to roll.

In the meantime toast the hazelnuts in the oven at 160°C for a few minutes. Once they have cooled completely, chop them finely.

When the chocolate ganache mixture is cool enough to work with, roll tablespoonfuls of the ganache into balls and roll with the chopped hazelnuts.

Makes 35 – 40

Lemon Cake with Aniseed and Dry Apricots

- 250 g butter, at room
  temperature
- grated rind of 2 lemons
- 500 ml castor sugar
- 6 eggs
- 570 ml flour
- ¼ tsp baking powder
- 250 ml cream
- 2.5 ml aniseed, crushed
- 100 g dry apricots, soaked
  in warm water and chopped
- 100 g flaked almonds

Preheat the oven to 160°C.

Cream the butter, lemon and sugar until soft, light
and fluffy. Add the eggs one at a time until well
incorporated. Combine the flours together and
add half the flour mixture and half the cream to the
butter mixture. Once well-combined add the rest of
the flour mixture, the rest of the cream, the aniseed
and the apricots.

Pour into a greased and lined cake tin of about
25 cm and garnish with the almonds.

Bake for about 1 ½ hours – this cake is very moist.

Serves 10 – 12

Baklava

- 500 g castor sugar
- 3 cardamom pods
- 1 kg blanched almonds
- 300 g honey
- 1 tsp ground cinnamon
- 500 g phyllo pastry
- 400 g butter, melted

Make the syrup by bringing the castor sugar, cardamom pods and 500 ml water to the boil. Once all the sugar has dissolved, turn the heat off.

In a food processor, blend the almonds with half the syrup, 100 g of honey and the cinnamon.

Using a tray 30 x 40 x 4 cm, layer 5 sheets of the phyllo pastry in the tray, brushing each layer generously with butter. Spread half of the almond mixture over one sheet of phyllo. Then layer another 5 sheets of phyllo with the butter each time.

Add the rest of the almond mixture. Finally layer the rest of the phyllo sheets, brushing with the butter each time. The top layer must be brushed with butter as well.

Put the tray in the fridge for a few hours so that it hardens. Once it is hard enough to handle cut the baklava into blocks using a sharp knife.

Bake the baklava at 170°C until golden brown and crisp. As soon as you take the baklava out the oven, pour the remaining syrup and honey over the top. Leave the baklava to cool completely before you take it out the tray and serve.

Makes about 100 blocks

ALMOND + ORANGE
FLORENTINES

R7 each

DATE BALLS

R4 each

...GUES

R4 each

INDEX

Besides boasting the title of being Tal's husband, **Russell Smith** is a passionate professional photographer, inspired by the city that surrounds him. A born Capetonian, he trained as an art director both here and in Paris, before turning his eye to photography. Russell works with either natural light, or with flash, but is always exacting about the details of a shoot. He has shot on location internationally – from Tuscany to Istanbul, from Mauritius to Botswana. Besides food, he shoots conceptual portraits, travel and studio stills.

Russell met his wife on a food shoot so it is no coincidence that one day they would work on a book together.

First published by Jacana Media (Pty) Ltd in 2013
Second and third impression 2014
Fourth impression 2015, Fifth impression 2016

10 Orange Street
Sunnyside
Auckland Park 2092
South Africa
+2711 628 3200
www.jacana.co.za

© text Tal Smith and Nikki Werner, 2013
© photography Russell Smith, 2013

ISBN 978-1-4314-0980-8

Design & layout by MR Design
Set in Futura & Garamond
Printed and bound by Creda Communications
Job no. 002496

See a complete list of Jacana titles at
www.jacana.co.za